AN

INTRODUCTION

TO THE

STUDY OF THE ROMAN LAW.

BY

LUTHER S. CUSHING.

William S. Hein & Co., Inc.
Buffalo, New York 14209
1989

LC 89-083502
ISBN 0-89941-686-1

The quality of materials reprinted is equivalent to the condition of the original work.

Printed in the United States of America.

This volume is printed on acid free paper by
WILLIAM S. HEIN & CO., INC.

AN

INTRODUCTION

TO THE

STUDY OF THE ROMAN LAW.

BY

LUTHER S. CUSHING.

BOSTON:
LITTLE, BROWN AND COMPANY.
MDCCCLIV.

RIVERSIDE, CAMBRIDGE:
PRINTED BY H. O. HOUGHTON AND COMPANY.

TO

THE MEMORY

OF THE LATE

JOHN PICKERING:

WHO, besides his eminence as a lawyer, was equally distinguished for his virtues as a man, for his accomplishments as a scholar, and for his cultivation and knowledge of general jurisprudence, the following pages are inscribed, as a testimonial of respect and affection, by

THE AUTHOR.

ADVERTISEMENT.

The following work was originally compiled as a short course of lectures on the Roman Law, and read before the Law School at Cambridge, in the second term of the academic year 1848 – 9. The plan of the course was, to select and treat chiefly of those topics, which, within the limited time devoted to this subject, would be of most advantage to the student. This object, it was thought, would be best accomplished by considering those points only in the history and present state of the science of Roman law, the knowledge of which would most readily enable the student to engage, at once, in the study of its principles.

In the execution of this purpose, the greatest attention was devoted to those matters which seemed most conducive to the end above stated;

leaving others of equal, or perhaps even of greater, interest, wholly or partially unnoticed.

In regard to that part of the course, which, from its nature, must necessarily be, to a considerable extent, a compilation, recourse has been had to those sources which are common to all, and the materials for it taken where they were most conveniently at hand. How far the general purpose has been advanced by the suggestion of any thing of my own, or how far the plan of the course has been successfully carried out, it is not for me to undertake to decide.

The object in view, namely, to furnish the student with the greatest amount of assistance, at the least possible expenditure of his time, will account for the extremely rudimentary nature of much of the original matter contained in the following pages, as well as for the general fact, that the whole work is rather suggestive, than full and exhausting, in its character.

The eighth chapter, in which the mode of referring to or citing the books of the Roman law is explained, is an exception to the foregoing remark, and will be found to afford all desirable information on the subject.

The lectures have been revised and published in their present form, not because they constitute a complete introduction to the study of the Roman law, but because they seem calculated, in some measure, to supply the present want of such a work for the use of the students of American law.

At the end of the volume will be found a table, alphabetically arranged, of the rubrics of all the titles of the institutes, digest, and code, with references to the compilation, and the number of the book and title, to which they belong. By the aid of this table, and of the explanations given in the eighth chapter, the place of any title can be found, when referred to, as is frequently the case, without its number, or the number of the book in which it is contained.

L. S. C.

BOSTON, April 1st, 1854.

TABLE OF CONTENTS.

The numbers refer to the paragraphs.

CHAPTER IV.

CHAPTER V.

CHAPTER VI.

CHAPTER VII.

CHAPTER VIII.

CHAPTER IX.

CHAPTER X.

APPENDIX.

STUDY OF THE ROMAN LAW.

CHAPTER I.

WHAT IS SIGNIFIED BY THE TERMS ROMAN LAW AND CIVIL LAW.

1. The terms Roman Law, and Civil Law, as commonly used, have various significations.

2. The terms Roman Law are sometimes used to denote all the remains of the law and jurisprudence of ancient Rome, of every description, and of every period, which have been preserved, and have come down, in any shape, to modern times.

3. By the Roman Law, we sometimes understand the legislation of Justinian, as embraced in the compilations made by his direction, a little before the middle of the sixth century, namely, The Institutes, Digest, Code, and Novels, or New Constitutions.

4. The terms Roman Law are sometimes used to denote the collection known as the *Corpus Juris Civilis*, which contains the legislation of Justinian,

above mentioned, together with certain other laws, all of which, together, constituted, at one period, the civil right or law of many of the nations of Europe. This collection being, for that reason, denominated the Body of Civil Right or Law, those terms have become synonymous with the Roman Law, and the latter is commonly known as the Civil Law.

5. In a still broader sense, the Roman Law embraces not only all the contents of the *Corpus Juris Civilis*, but all the works of every description,—glosses, commentaries, institutes, or by whatever name they are called,—which have been written on the subject, since the Roman Law, as compiled by Justinian, became established, as a basis of civil right.

6. The terms Civil Law are sometimes used to denote the law and jurisprudence of those countries which have adopted the Roman law, and the jurists of such countries are called the civilians. It is in this sense, that subjects are sometimes referred to as coming under the Roman law, which only belong to the law and jurisprudence of those countries in which the Roman law prevails, but which have little or nothing to do with the Roman law itself. Thus, it is frequently said in the books, that, by the civil law, or according to the civilians, such or such would be the rule in a given case; by which it is not necessarily to be understood, that the text of the Roman law is referred to, but only the opinion or decision of jurists learned in that law.

7. In the year 533 of the Christian era, nearly

thirteen centuries from the foundation of the city of Rome, the great work of legislation, undertaken by the emperor Justinian, was completed and promulgated. The purpose of this undertaking was to reduce the great mass of the laws, then existing, into order, and to make them known to the people. This revision is the only authentic and acknowledged source of the Roman law in use in modern times; and, therefore, as possessing the highest interest for the student of law, will receive the greatest share of his attention.

8. The Roman law is a subject so intimately connected with history, with political science, with philology, and even with criticism, that a volume might well be employed in treating of the relations which it bears to these topics.

9. But it is in neither of these relations, that the Roman law has much, if any, interest for the practical lawyer, or that it is of much, if of any, value, as a branch of professional education. This system is, to a considerable extent, the basis of the legal polity of continental Europe, and of some of the states of America; and many of its principles have been adopted in the common law of England, and of this country. It is with reference chiefly to these relations, that it will be found useful and even necessary to obtain some knowledge of the imperial jurisprudence.

10. A complete and thorough course of Roman law, according to the emperor Justinian, required

five years for its completion. A less period would doubtless suffice, for the same purpose, at the present day. But, however much the term for its accomplishment might be reduced, it would still be found to be wholly impracticable, within the limits of a brief introduction, intended for the use of the professional student, and adapted to the time at his command, to go through with any thing even approaching to a complete survey of this science.

11. Considering, then, that a thorough knowledge of it is entirely out of the question, as a branch of preliminary education in this country, two alternatives remain; either to present a general and brief outline of the system, or to explain so much and such parts of it, as to enable the student to prosecute the study further, if he may think proper. The latter course, there can be no doubt, will be altogether the most advantageous. It will be the purpose of this introduction, therefore, not so much to explore the vast field of the Roman law, as to point out the way by which the student of jurisprudence may do it for himself.

12. In order to obtain an adequate idea of the Roman law, as contained in the imperial compilations, it will be necessary, in the first place, to trace its history anterior to Justinian ; secondly, to give an account of the revision of the Roman law by his direction ; thirdly, to trace its history since Justinian ; and, lastly, it will be useful to advert to the plan of the several works, which are now the only authentic

sources of this system, with a view to explain their mechanical structure, and the different methods of citing or referring to their contents. In the execution of the plan thus suggested, it will be necessary to assume, that, to some extent, at least, the reader is acquainted with the general history of Rome, with that of the Middle Ages, and with the modern history of Europe.

CHAPTER II.

DISTINCTION BETWEEN LEGISLATION AND JURISPRUDENCE.

13. By way of introduction to the subject, it is proposed to call attention to a distinction which is very little adverted to in the ordinary use of legal language, but which is quite important to be fully comprehended, in order to a proper understanding, or to a due appreciation, of the Roman law. The distinction alluded to is that which exists between Legislation and Jurisprudence, or, in other words, between the laws, properly so called, and their application to particular cases.

14. In every civilized community, however low in the scale it may stand, there is an absolute and an indispensable necessity that justice should be administered; a necessity so absolute and so indispensable, that, unless provided for by some recognized authority, each individual of the community will attempt to administer justice for himself. This necessity lies at the very foundation of civil society. All social institutions, whether political, or legal, have this for their immediate object. The constitution of the United States declares, that one of the prin-

cipal purposes, for which it was ordained, was "to establish justice;" and that of Massachusetts asserts, that it is essential to the preservation of the rights of every individual, that there should be "an impartial interpretation of the laws, and administration of justice."

15. What, then, is it that we understand by the administration of justice? "Justice," says the Roman jurist Ulpian, "is the constant and perpetual disposition to render every man his due." To administer justice, therefore, is to compel every one to be in, and to live according to, this constant and perpetual disposition. But no man can be in this disposition, or live according to it, unless he knows what it is that is due from him to others; and this knowledge necessarily presupposes the existence of certain rules, by which every one is bound to govern and regulate his conduct towards every other.

16. The rules, by which the members of a community are thus required to conduct themselves, are generally found existing, to a greater or less extent, in some authentic form, either as written laws, or as acknowledged customs and usages. But this form is not necessary to their existence or their authority. They need not be formally agreed upon, or reduced to writing, or even promulgated. Whenever human beings live together in a state of society, that fact alone brings into existence certain laws by which they must so live, establishes the authority of

those laws, and subjects all the members of the community to their dominion. The rules of conduct, which are thus coeval with society, are denominated the precepts of natural right. The same great jurist, already referred to, reduces them to these three: "to live honestly, to hurt no one, to give to every man his due."

17. In a community, in which there were no other rules for the government of the members, than these precepts of natural right, — and this is probably the case in all communities, for a longer or shorter period, during the infancy of their existence, — if any member should fail in the observance of these precepts, the universal sense of justice, implanted in the hearts of all men, would instantly require, that the delinquent should be compelled to do what he ought to have done voluntarily, or that he should place the party, who had been injured by his delinquency, in the same situation in which he would have been, or as nearly as may be thereto, if the precepts of natural law, which he has neglected or broken, had been observed. This is what justice, — that is, the constant and perpetual disposition to render every man his due, — requires should be done; and the doing of this, under whatever form it may take place, is what is meant by the administration of justice. The knowledge, that justice will be done, or enforced, is the only external security that men shall conduct themselves according to its precepts; and thus the administration of justice is an absolute and an

indispensable necessity, in every civilized community.

18. From what has just been stated, it is apparent, that the purpose of human law is twofold: first, to regulate the conduct of men living in a state of society, towards one another; and, second, when its precepts are violated or disregarded, to ascertain the relations of right which have been thus disturbed, with a view to their reëstablishment; or, in other words, law is the rule of civil conduct, and also the measure of justice.

19. If, in such a community as we have supposed the existence of, it should be found necessary or expedient to have further or more specific rules for the civil conduct of its members, which should be introduced accordingly, those rules would become the measure of right and of justice, for all cases and circumstances to which they should apply, leaving all other cases and circumstances to be governed, as before, by the precepts of natural right. The introduction of such new rules has hitherto been found essential to the progress of society, and marks its advancement in civilization.

20. The rules of conduct, which are thus expressly adopted, from time to time, for the government of a community, are denominated its laws. They constitute, as already remarked, the rules of right and the measure of justice, for all cases to which they refer, and so far supersede the rules of natural right. But in all other respects, the precepts of natural right

remain in full force, and are never in fact entirely superseded, either as rules of conduct, or as the measure of justice, by the provisions, however numerous, of positive legislation. This is apparent, in the first place, from the obvious principle, that the original laws of a community can only be abrogated by the introduction of new ones, by which the former are superseded, in reference to the same subject-matter; and, in the second place, from the impossibility, equally obvious, that human foresight should ever anticipate, or human wisdom provide for, the infinite variety of human conduct.

21. It is thus apparent, that the laws of every community consist of these two elements; first, those rules of conduct which are introduced by the law-making power, in an express and positive form, for the particular circumstances and cases to which they relate; and, second, those precepts of natural right, which are not superseded by the former, and which therefore remain in full force as to all other circumstances and cases. The latter are authoritative from the first moment of the existence of the community in which they prevail; the former first become authoritative, or, in other words, are introduced, in two different modes, — namely, by legislation, properly so called, and by usage or custom.

22. Laws, therefore, considered with reference to the manner of their introduction, are of three kinds; first, legislative acts; second, customs or usages; and, third, the precepts of natural right.

23. The *first* consists of acts or declarations emanating directly from the law-making power, in the authentic and established form, and purporting to be rules of conduct in the circumstances, and for the cases, to which they relate. Such acts of legislation are either general or special. Of the former, the legislation of the Twelve Tables, in the history of the Roman republic, and the frequent revisions of the statute laws, and other forms of codification, at the present day, are examples. To the latter class belong the particular laws which, from time to time, proceeded from the people, and from the senate of Rome, during the republic; from the emperors, after the republic was destroyed; and from the legislative bodies of modern times.

24. The *second* kind of laws consists of customs and usages, which, being generally known, assented to, and observed, have thereby acquired the force, and received the name, of laws. A great number of the laws, both of ancient and modern times, rest only on this foundation.

25. The *third* class of laws is composed of those principles or precepts of natural right, which have never been superseded by express legislation. The principles, which are thus left in the midst of positive law, are, in general, those fundamental principles which are necessarily presupposed by every code, and by every act of legislation, general or special, unless abrogated in express terms, with reference to certain particular and excepted cases; such,

for example, as the precept, that no man shall be the judge in his own cause.[1]

---

[1] The case of *Scott* v. *Dickinson*, 14 Pick. 276, furnishes an apt illustration of the principle stated in the text. In that case, it appeared, that by a statute (*St.* 1785, *c.* 52,) in Massachusetts, regulating the proceedings between adjoining proprietors of land, with regard to the making of the partition fence between them, it was provided, amongst other things, that if one of them should neglect to make his part within the time fixed, the other might do it at his own expense, and recover of the delinquent proprietor his proportion thereof, (doubled in amount,) upon the adjudication of two or more of the fence-viewers that the fence was sufficient. The plaintiff had made the whole fence between him and the defendant, pursuant to the requisitions of the statute, and brought his action against the latter to recover his share of the expense. He had obtained an adjudication of the fence-viewers, according to the statute, but without giving any notice to the defendant of the time and place of their proceeding, which was not required by the statute. The Court held, that the action could not be maintained. SHAW, C. J., after stating the case, said: — "It is found, in the present case, that such an adjudication was made, but it is found that no notice of the time and place of assessing this amount or valuation was given to the defendant. The statute does not in terms require such a notice, but we think it does by reasonable and necessary implication. As a general rule and principle of justice, whenever persons are appointed to arbitrate and adjudicate upon the rights of others, some notice is to be given to enable each party to state his claims and views, and to adduce pertinent and proper proofs. And there seems to be a peculiar propriety in adhering to this rule, where the full amount of an actual indemnity is to be doubled by way of penalty. Where it is intended by the legislature, that referees, arbitrators, commissioners, or other like bodies, appointed to pass judgment upon the rights of others, shall have power to proceed *ex parte*, such an intent should be manifested in express terms, or by necessary implication." So, upon the same principle, it was held, that selectmen in Massachusetts were not authorized by *St.* 1783, *c.* 38, § 5, to proceed to the appointment of a guardian to one as a lunatic or *non compos*, without giving notice to the party, that he might be heard on the question,

26. The laws of all civilized communities are composed of these three elements; not in equal proportions, nor, probably, in any two states, in the same proportions. In some, where the law-making power has been the most active, the great mass of the laws consists of acts of positive legislation. In others, the customary law prevails to the greatest extent. In others, again, the precepts of natural right will be found to predominate.

27. The term Legislation, though ordinarily restricted, in its signification, to the act of making a law, or a code of laws, is sometimes used to denote the whole body of legislative acts, of whatever name or origin, and may not improperly be extended to embrace the entire mass of what are denominated laws, taken collectively. It is in this latter sense, that it is here distinguished from Jurisprudence.

28. Having thus explained what is meant by Legislation, the meaning of the term Jurisprudence will now be considered.

29. The *primary* purpose of a system or code of laws, such as has just been described, is to provide those who are subject to its jurisdiction with rules of conduct by which to govern themselves in all those affairs of life, which may become the subjects of legal relations. If these rules are duly observed, the purpose of the law will be accomplished, and

---

whether such appointment was necessary or proper, although no notice or hearing was required by the statute. *Chase* v. *Hathaway*, 14 Mass. 222.

it will have no further object. But this not being always the case, — the rules of civil conduct being sometimes violated or disregarded, — it then becomes the *secondary* purpose of the law, to furnish rules for determining what legal rights and duties have been thus violated, and what ought to be done, in order that those whose legal relations are disturbed may be placed, as near as may be, in the same situation in which they would have stood, if the rules of civil conduct had been observed. The law then becomes the measure of justice.

30. In order to explain this distinction, let us suppose, for example, that it is a principle or precept of the law, that contracts, legally made, shall be performed, and that two individuals enter into such a contract, the one to sell, and the other to buy, a particular thing, for an agreed price. The precept of law, which is the rule of conduct, immediately applies to the relations between the parties, and requires them to do what they have thus agreed to do. This is the primary object of the law. If either party refuses or neglects to perform the contract, on his part, the other invokes the aid of the civil magistrate, and, upon the facts of the case being established, the law is at once applied to it, and the party in fault is compelled to do what he ought to have done, in the first instance, according to the terms of his contract, or its equivalent, if that has become impossible. If, for example, the default is on the part of the seller, who refuses to deliver the thing and receive the price,

the law compels him to do so, and to compensate the buyer for any injury he may have suffered in consequence of the delay. If the seller has sold and delivered the thing to another person; or if, for any other cause, it is no longer in his power to deliver it, the buyer will be entitled to receive a compensation for the injury he has sustained in damages. This is the secondary purpose of the law.

31. If it were in the power of the human mind to foresee, and to provide rules beforehand to regulate, the conduct of men in every variety of circumstances and conditions, then, when individuals violated or neglected the rules thus prescribed, the departure from right would be immediately recognized, and the rules to be applied, in order to restore the legal relations of the parties, would at once become manifest. In the administration of justice, under such a system, it would only be necessary, first, to ascertain the facts; second, to direct the party in fault to do what the law requires at his hands, for the benefit of the party injured, or its equivalent; and, third, to take the necessary measures to compel obedience to such directions.

32. This may be illustrated by taking, as an example, a case in which all the circumstances are foreseen and provided for by the law.[1] Let us suppose, then, that the law prescribes as a rule of con-

[1] A single case in which all the circumstances are foreseen is supposable; although a system equally complete, — present and prospective, — is not to be imagined.

duct, that contracts legally made shall be performed; but with this exception, among others, that where a contract is entered into between a person of full age and a minor, the contract shall only be binding on the latter, so far as it may be beneficial to him. The law has also determined what the precise age is, which separates minority from majority, and has enumerated all the contracts which are to be regarded as beneficial to minors, at every period of their minority. These provisions are the rules of conduct by which parties ought to govern themselves, when in the circumstances and situation contemplated by the law. If we suppose, now, that a contract is entered into between a person of full age and a minor, with reference to a matter which the law declares to be beneficial to the latter, we shall have a case, in relation to which, and to every part of which, the law has made particular provision for the government and direction of the parties. If the minor refuses or neglects to perform the contract on his part, then, when the fact is ascertained, the law immediately and at once applies to the case, and furnishes the rule by which justice is to be done between the parties.

33. But it is not in the power of human intelligence to foresee and provide beforehand for every combination of facts or circumstances, which may occur in the infinite variety of human affairs. No human code ever undertook to do this. No human wisdom could have accomplished such a task, if it had ever been undertaken. The law-maker, how-

ever desirous he may be to make his code complete, can only foresee and provide for classes of cases; and, in doing this, he must rather be guided by the experience of the past, than by any faculty of discerning the future.

34. There is, accordingly, a large class of cases which are inevitably left unprovided for by every system of human legislation; and it becomes an interesting inquiry to determine, what are the rules of conduct, and what is the measure of justice, in reference to such cases. The answer has already been indicated, when speaking of legislation. It is, that the laws, applicable to such cases, are those precepts of natural right, which have not been superseded by express legislation. If a case is left wholly unprovided for by the positive law, it is governed solely by the natural law; if in part only, then partly by the natural and partly by the positive law. The natural law thus becomes the complement of positive legislation, and supplies its deficiencies, in reference to all cases which are either wholly, or in part only, regulated by its provisions.

35. In order to explain this by an example, let us suppose the case already imagined, leaving out one of its elements. The law, we will suppose, provides, that contracts legally made shall be performed; that minors shall only be bound to perform their contracts so far as such contracts are for their advantage; and that persons under a certain age are minors; but the law does not specify what contracts are, and what

are not, beneficial to them. If, in this state of the law, a contract is entered into between a minor and a person of full age, we will suppose, for example, for the cure of the former of a dangerous disease, and for the payment of a reasonable sum therefor, by the minor, it is clear, that the law furnishes in part only, in express terms, the rule by which the parties are to govern themselves, and in part only the rule by which justice is to be administered. It is silent with respect to one important element, in both, namely, the nature of the contract; it has not declared what contracts are, and what are not, beneficial to minors; that must be determined by a reference to some other source than the terms of the law; and it must be ascertained, before either the primary or the secondary purpose of the law can be effected.

36. We see, at once, that besides ascertaining the facts, it is necessary also to find out and establish those rules of natural right, which are the complement of the positive law, in this respect, and which serve to connect it with the particular case, that is to say, the rules by which to determine whether the contract is one of a beneficial nature, or otherwise; and thus, whether it ought or ought not to be executed by the minor. The process which we have now to perform is to ascertain what the legislator himself would have enacted, if he had undertaken to carry out the law in detail; or, in other words, what is right and just, with reference to the matter in question, it not being supposable that the legislator would have ordained otherwise in any case.

37. In order to do this, in cases like the one supposed, it may be necessary, besides considering the general condition of minority, to take into view all the circumstances of the minor's situation, such, for example, as his rank in life, his precise age, his property, his education, state of health, whether or not he has a father or other guardian, whether or not he is married. Having duly considered all the circumstances, we establish what we deem to be right in the particular case; for example, that the contract is a beneficial one, and ought to be performed; and thus we supply the deficiency resulting from the generality of the terms in which the law is expressed. What is so decided, becomes a rule of conduct, or a measure of justice in the particular case; and, if established by a court of justice, a precedent for similar cases subsequently occurring. In this process, a new principle of right relative to contracts has been developed, namely, that the contract of a minor, to pay for his cure of a dangerous disease, is a beneficial one, and to be performed.

38. In order to illustrate the subject still further, let us now suppose another case, arising after the decision of the preceding. Assuming the law to be as before stated, with reference to contracts in general, and also with reference to the contracts of minors, and assuming that it has been authoritatively established, that the contract of a minor to pay for his cure is a beneficial one, and ought to be performed, the case we now suppose contains a further fact,

namely, that the minor has a father who has already provided him with the necessary medical attendance, and that this was known to the person with whom the contract was made. Upon this state of facts, it is decided, that the contract in question is not beneficial to the minor, and ought not to be performed. This decision, like the former, establishes a new principle, relative to the law of contracts, and becomes a precedent for future cases. Let us now suppose a third case, subsequently occurring, which varies from the last only in this, that, instead of a father, the minor has a guardian, by whom he is provided with the necessary medical attendance. In this case, as the relation which subsists between guardian and ward, so far as the care and support of the latter are concerned, is the same as between parent and child, it is decided, that the same reason applies in this as in the former case, and consequently, that the contract is not beneficial to the minor. A third principle, relative to the law of contracts, is thus developed and established.

39. It will be perceived, on reviewing the examples which we have just supposed, for the purpose of illustration, that we started in the first place with two principles of law or legislation, namely, that contracts are to be performed, and that minors are to be exempted from the performance of those which are not beneficial to them; and that in applying these principles to particular cases, we have developed three others relative to the same subject, namely,

1st, that a contract by a minor to pay for his cure of a dangerous disease is a beneficial contract; unless, 2d, he have a father, or, 3d, a guardian, by whom he is provided with all necessary medical attendance. The principles, thus developed and established, in the practical application of the law, properly so called, constitute what is denominated Jurisprudence.

40. Principles of jurisprudence, as above described, become developed in two ways, or forms. The first occurs when a question arises in the mind of an individual, as to what the law requires him to do in a particular case. When this happens, the party either determines for himself what he ought to do, or he applies for information to some other person, who makes it a business or profession to consider and advise in such matters. The principles, which are thus developed, gradually assume the character of usages, and become a part of the customary law. The second form, in which jurisprudence is developed, occurs in the administration of justice. The cases, which are decided in this way, become precedents or authorities for similar and analogous cases subsequently occurring.

41. Legislation being the establishment, beforehand, of those general principles by which civil conduct is to be regulated, and Jurisprudence consisting of those principles which are developed in the application of the former to particular cases, it follows, that the latter will be more or less extensive, accord-

ing as the former is more or less general or particular; jurisprudence being most extensive where the law is most general, and least extensive where the law goes the furthest into details and particulars. Legislation, though usually general, may nevertheless descend to minute details and particulars. When this is the case, it so far occupies the place which would otherwise be filled by jurisprudence. Jurisprudence, on the other hand, supplying all that legislation leaves unprovided for, in the administration of justice, and developing principles which serve as rules of conduct for cases subsequently arising, so far stands in the place and performs the functions of legislation.

42. Jurisprudence is, therefore, the complement of Legislation; it supplies what is left unprovided for by the latter, in the administration of justice; and the two together constitute the Legal Polity of a state.

43. Although it may be stated generally, that it is the province of legislation to provide general rules, and the province of jurisprudence to apply those rules to particular cases, and that this is in fact the practical distinction between them; yet it would be difficult, either by reference to codes, ancient or modern, or by any *à priori* reasoning, to establish the precise boundary which separates the one from the other, and to attribute to each the exact domain to which it is appropriately entitled. An examination of codes and systems would probably show, that the

great outlines, embracing those institutions which are peculiar to each, and which, to a certain extent, are political in their character, have been the work of legislation; while those parts which have their foundation in natural justice, and are the same, or nearly so, among all nations of the same rank in civilization, and which chiefly affect the relations of the citizens to one another, have been the product of jurisprudence.

44. The great and essential difference between Legislation and Jurisprudence, that which separates the one from the other distinctly, is the manner in which they respectively become established. The former takes place when the law-making power discovers occasion for it; and its provisions are framed prospectively for such classes of cases as the legislator thinks most likely to occur. The latter is only called into being when an actual case arises for its exercise, and is then adapted to the particular circumstances of that case. Legislation, when once established, becomes fixed and unalterable, and receives no additions, but by subsequent legislation. Jurisprudence is constantly progressive, and continually enlarging and extending itself, as cases occur for its exercise, and adapting its principles to the social and political changes which are perpetually going on in society.

45. The acts of the legislative power being fixed and unalterable but by itself, and the principles of jurisprudence increasing and expanding with the

administration of justice, it may happen, that if the former lies dormant for a long period, or is inadequate to the wants of society, that the legislation, properly so called, of a nation, may become wholly or partially superseded by its jurisprudence. The latter first supplies what is wanting to the former; gradually the provisions of the law become obsolete; and then jurisprudence takes their place altogether. The process, by which this is accomplished, is continually taking place, to a greater or less extent, in every country, and at all times. In Rome, at the time of Justinian, of which we shall speak presently, legislation, properly so called, had become to a considerable extent superseded by jurisprudence.

46. An important difference between legislation and jurisprudence, resulting from the different modes in which they become established, manifests itself in the nature and character of the principles of which they respectively consist. Legislation is, for the most part, the expression of the popular sentiment, for the time being, providing for the future by the experience of the past; it may be, and often is, injuriously affected by the nature of the occasion which calls for it; it may, and often does, take place under the influence and for the advantage of a party or a faction; it depends for its authority chiefly upon the power which enacts it; and it is not necessarily the work of persons endowed with the requisite skill and knowledge. Jurisprudence, on the contrary, assumes only to provide for actual cases as they oc-

cur, and arrives only at right and justice in each particular case, having due regard to the established law, and to the great and leading principles of right; it is established under no other influence than a desire to do justice, and for the advantage of one who is entitled to justice; it is ordinarily the work of persons whose lives are devoted to its pursuit and study, and who possess all the skill and knowledge of the age; it depends for its sanction only upon the sense of justice which exists in the community; and it is susceptible of modification, from time to time, to adapt it to the varying wants of society. It is hardly necessary to observe, that principles thus developed and established, within their appropriate sphere, are more likely to be founded in right, and more certain to effect justice, than the precepts of ordinary legislation.

47. The distinction between law and jurisprudence, which it has thus been attempted to explain, within the compass of a few paragraphs, would require a volume, rather than a chapter, for its full elucidation. If the attempt has succeeded in making the subject intelligible, the assertion will be comprehended at once, that it is mainly as a system of jurisprudence, as distinguished from legislation, that the Roman law is entitled to the highest veneration, — that it has for ages received the most profound attention of learned men and jurists, — and that it is now worthy to be studied as a branch of professional education. Other nations of anti-

quity have had their codes and systems of law, some of which, perhaps, may have been equal, if not superior to the Roman legislation ; but no other nation possessed or preserved a written jurisprudence.[1]

48. In modern times, the jurisprudence of the common law of England, under which is embraced, of course, that of this country, stands preëminent for the extent and variety of the topics which it embraces, the thoroughness of its investigations, and the wisdom of its decisions. The great jurists of Rome dealt with the rudiments of legal science, and their names will be forever associated with the principles on which it rests. But, while we concede to the Roman jurists the honorable preëminence of being the first in point of time, we cannot refuse to the great jurists of England and America the high distinction of being their equals in point of merit. If the former were the founders of a legal polity, which had no equal in antiquity, the latter have built up a system, which has no superior in modern times.

---

[1] "The merits of the Roman jurists did not consist in making a systematic arrangement of the whole matter of law, though they have done much towards helping us to make it. Their merit lay in their skilful application of principles to the resolving of particular cases, in which they display a rectitude of purpose, a happy brevity of expression, and a mastery of their matter, that have commanded the admiration of all competent judges, and furnish the best models for our imitation." Long's Discourses, 26.

CHAPTER III.

HISTORY OF ROMAN LEGISLATION ANTERIOR TO THE TIME OF JUSTINIAN.

49. IN tracing the history of the Roman Law, prior to the time of Justinian, the chief purpose in view will be to become acquainted with the state and condition in which it was when his revision was effected; or, in other words, with the various materials of which his work was composed. When we have obtained some knowledge of these materials, and of the manner in which they were dealt with by him, we shall then be in a situation to study the doctrines which his compilations contain.

50. The history of the Roman law, during this earlier period, has been sketched by Pomponius, one of the authors whose writings compose the Digest, and who lived about a century and a half before the Christian era. His account will be substantially followed, in the brief notice which it is proposed now to give.[1]

---

[1] Digest, Book 1, Tit. 2. *De origine juris, et omnium magistratuum, et successione prudentium:*—"Of the origin of right, and of all magis-

51. The earliest written collection of laws, of which there is any account, is denominated the *Papirian Law*, from the name of the compiler, Sextus Papirius, who is supposed to have lived in the time of the elder Tarquin, and to have made a collection of the laws of that king and his predecessors. Of this collection, a single fragment has been preserved,[1] and it is mentioned once in the Digest.[2]

52. Servius Tullius, who succeeded Tarquin, made several useful laws, among which were laws relating to imprisonment for debt, — a fruitful subject in the earlier Roman legislation, — and for the protection of the weaker citizens against the stronger.

53. After the expulsion of the kings, all the laws which had been enacted by them, were abolished by the establishment of the power of the tribunes of the people, or, as Pomponius expresses it, by the tribunitian law. Several of the laws thus abrogated, — probably those which referred to matters of private right, and were not political in their character, — continued to be observed as usages. This state of things, which seems to have given occasion to much abuse and oppression, was succeeded, after some time, by the first great act of Roman legislation, the

---

trates, and of the succession of the jurisconsults." This title consists of but two fragments, the last of which, containing the history, is taken from a work of Pomponius, entitled *Enchiridium*, or Manual, and is divided into forty-seven sections.

[1] See Blondeau's Institutes de l' Empereur Justinien, II. 76.

[2] Dig. 50, 16, *De Verb. Sign.* 144.

establishment of the Laws of the Twelve Tables, about the year 300 of Rome, or 450 years before the common era.

54. From this time, the important distinction, adverted to in the last chapter, becomes apparent in the several branches or sources of the Roman law; which it is proposed accordingly to consider, under the two general heads of Legislation and Jurisprudence.

55. The Legislation, properly so called, from the commencement of the republic to the time of Justinian, consists: — 1, of the Laws of the Twelve Tables; 2, of the Laws enacted by the People; 3, of the Laws enacted by the Senate; and, 4, of the Laws of the Emperors, or Imperial Constitutions.

SECTION I. — *The Laws of the Twelve Tables.*

56. The most remarkable feature of early Roman history is the division of the people into two different classes, the patricians and the plebeians, living together upon somewhat unequal terms, and the consequent struggles which ensued, and which were continually occurring, between them. The patricians were the aristocracy. From their ranks the priests and the principal magistrates were taken. To them belonged the functions of government. It is no new truth, but as old as the Roman republic, at least, that the possession of power engenders its abuse. The

oppressions of the patricians more than once induced revolt on the part of the plebeians, and threatened the destruction of the state.

57. It is not to be supposed, however, from the existence of this distinction, and the attribution of rights and privileges to one class, which were denied to the other, that any such relation subsisted between them as that of master and slave, or that the plebeians were a class analogous to the modern serfs of Russia, or the ancient villeins and bondmen of England. The distinction between them was probably more like that which prevails in some of the other nations of modern Europe, between the nobility and peasantry. It was not a relation in which there was the right of absolute control on the one hand, and the duty of implicit submission on the other; but a relation which was founded in, and regulated by, the law; and in which, if the parties did not stand upon a footing of equality, each of them nevertheless possessed rights, and was subject to duties, which were protected and enforced by a law common to both. If distinctions were made between them by the law, those distinctions were acquiesced in and submitted to by the plebeians, in view of advantages, which, in some form or other, were probably regarded as a full equivalent. Upon no other supposition, can the fact be explained, that these distinctions were kept up for so long a period;[1] especially, when it is recol-

[1] In the year of the city 261, the plebeians obtained a complete political equality with the patricians, and after the year 303, intermarriages between the two classes were permitted.

lected that the plebeians were the most numerous, and that they constituted, probably, a great majority of the soldiery.

58. After the expulsion of the kings, and the abrogation of the royal laws, the consular government was established, and the people were for some time left without the written laws to which they had been so long accustomed under the kings. This condition of things appears to have been taken advantage of by the magistrates, who were all of the patrician rank, and were not unwilling, for the sake of advancing the interests of their order, to oppress and harass the plebeians. The evil became at length so intolerable, that the plebeians demanded, and ultimately compelled the patricians to concede, that measures should be taken for compiling a code of laws, which, being certain and known, should guarantee the civil rights of the people, against the oppression of their magistrates.

59. The first step towards the preparation and enactment of the new code, was the sending of three of the senators to Greece,[1] for the purpose of obtaining a knowledge of the laws and institutions of Athens, and other states. On their return, ten commissioners were appointed to prepare the code. The plebeians struggled hard for an equal representation with the patricians, on the commission, but, after some time, they gave up the point, and the com-

---

[1] Dr. Arnold mentions the embassy to Greece without question.

missioners were all taken from the patrician order.

60. After the appointment of the commissioners, the functions of all the ordinary magistrates were suspended, and the commissioners were invested with the supreme powers of government, during the time they should be employed in their work. This was done, according to Pomponius, in order that the commissioners might put in force and interpret the laws which they should make, and might modify and correct them, if they should find it necessary.

61. The commissioners, having in a few months drawn up a plan for a code, caused it to be engraved on ten tables, and set up in a conspicuous place for the inspection of the people, who were invited to make known such corrections as they desired to have made, which were considered and adopted, so far as they met the approbation of the commissioners. At the end of a year, the new code was completed, and, having received the sanction of the senate, and of the people, became the established law. The laws thus made were engraved on ten tablets of brass, which were set up in the *comitium*, for the information and direction of all the citizens. The people were so well pleased with the government of the decemvirs, as the commissioners were called, and with the new laws, that it was determined to continue the same form of government another year. Accordingly, ten commissioners, only

one of whom had been on the first board, were appointed for the second year, by whom two tables more were compiled, and added to the ten already in force. The new code then received the name of the Laws of the Twelve Tables.

62. "It cannot be doubted," says Dr. Arnold,[1] "that the ten tables were a complete work, and intended to be so by their authors. All the circumstances of their enactment show this; it seems shown, also, by their number, which had reference to that of the ten commissioners, as if each commissioner had contributed an equal portion to their joint work. It is clear, also, that they satisfied the expectations of the people, and were drawn up in a spirit of fairness and wisdom; for whatever the Romans found fault with in the laws of the twelve tables was contained in the two last of them, and the laws, as a whole, are spoken of with high admiration, and remained for centuries as the foundation of all the Roman law."

63. In order to satisfy the demands of the people, it was necessary that the new code should contain a body of fundamental laws, such as we are accustomed at the present day to call a constitution, as well as laws for regulating the rights and duties of the citizens towards each other; and it seems that both these objects, at least to a great extent, were

---

1 Arnold's History of Rome, I. 256.

accomplished. The laws of the twelve tables may consequently be considered, not only as a revision of the legal polity of Rome, but as a sort of constitutional compact between the different orders, by which the rights of each and of all were established and guaranteed.

64. There is one further feature in the laws of the twelve tables, which deserves to be mentioned. The history of the proceedings, relative to their enactment, shows that they are to be regarded as a concession, on the part of the patricians, to a demand made by the plebeians, with which concession the latter agreed to be content. We should expect, therefore, that the patricians would yield as little as possible, and that the plebeians would demand as much as there was any probability of their obtaining. We should expect, also, that when the code came to be put in operation, the patricians, who still continued to fill all the offices of the magistracy, would endeavor on their part to do all in their power to turn the administration of justice to the benefit of their order; and that the plebeians, on their part, would insist that the laws, for which they had struggled so manfully, should be faithfully administered, with an equal regard for the rights of all.

65. We shall find, doubtless, if we consider in detail the system of jurisprudence which grew up under the laws of the twelve tables, that some of its most peculiar and striking characteristics are to be

attributed to the conflicts of the description alluded to, which, for a considerable period, continued to occur between the two orders.

66. The legislation of the decemvirs, at the time of Justinian, had become so entirely superseded by the jurisprudence of several centuries, that it existed only in fragments, as quoted or referred to by ancient authors. Several attempts have been made to reconstruct these laws from the fragments which remain; the most recent and successful of which are by Haubold,[1] and by Dirksen.[2] The latter, which is the most complete, contains, also, an elaborate review of all the preceding works on the subject.

67. Enough has already been said to indicate, in general, the contents of this celebrated code. In point of form, its provisions are most remarkable for the brevity and conciseness with which they are expressed. This extreme brevity has been made a ground of reproach, as if it was intended for the very purpose of leaving scope for comment and interpretation; thus depriving the people of one of the chief benefits which they expected to derive from the new legislation. But this reproach is no doubt entirely gratuitous. Sufficient reasons for their brevity may be found in the character of the laws, the purpose

---

[1] *Institutionum Juris Romani Privati Lineamenta*, as republished after his death by Dr. Otto, Leipzig, 1826.

[2] Leipzig, 1824.

for which they were framed, and the manner of their promulgation; without imputing to the decemvirs any such bad faith as is implied in the charge of intentional obscurity.

68. In order to give some idea of the laws of the twelve tables, the following translation of those contained in the first table, as restored by Dirksen and Zell, will be found sufficient. This table is entitled *De in Jus*[1] *Vocando*, that is, of citation in justice, and, as restored, is composed of nine short paragraphs, eight of which are as follows: —

1. "If any one cites another *in jus*, and the party cited does not follow, let the former take witnesses, and then bring the latter before the magistrate."

2. "If and then the party cited delays, or attempts flight, let the other lay hands on him."

3. "If the party cited is prevented from going by sickness or old age, let the other party provide him with a vehicle drawn by cattle. If the party citing, upon demand made by the party cited, is unwilling, he cannot be compelled, to provide him with a covered carriage."

4. "Let the bail (*vindex*)[2] for a rich man be rich; for a poor man any one that offers."

---

[1] The word *Jus*, as used in reference to legal proceedings, was opposed to the word *Judicium;* a thing being said to be done *in jure*, or *in judicio*, according as it was done before the magistrate, or before a *judex;* thus, summoning one to appear before the *prætor* was called *in jus vocatio*, and the subsequent proceedings, before the *judex*, were said to be *in judicio*.

[2] The *Vindex* was some responsible person procured by the defend-

5. " If, while the parties are on the way, the affair is settled (*transactum*) between them, let it be so established."

6. " If the affair is not settled on the way, then let the prætor, in the *comitium* or *forum*, before noon, both parties being present, take cognizance of the cause, and hear them fully."

7. "After noon, although one of the parties only is present, let the prætor give him an action and institute legal proceedings in his favor."

8. "At sunset let there be an end of judicial proceedings." [1]

69. These paragraphs are all that remain of the contents of the first table. Their style and character afford a good idea of the whole. The remains of the other tables are many of them greater in quantity; one or two of them less; so that we may probably judge very nearly of the magnitude of the whole work, by supposing twelve tables somewhat larger than what remains of the first.[2]

---

ant, on his way to the prætor, to undertake his defence. See *post*, 114.

[1] Elemens de Droit Romain par Heineccius; Introduction Historique par M. Ch. de Giraud, à Paris, 1835. The restoration, by Dirksen and Zell, is printed as an appendix to the above entitled work. See also Blondeau's Institutes, II. 61.

[2] The legislation of the twelve tables is described by Niebuhr, Vol. II. Am. ed. p. 232; Schmitz, ch. viii.; Dr. Arnold's History of Rome, Vol. I. ch. xiv. and xv. The latter is the most satisfactory. Milman, in a note to Gibbon, Vol. V. (Lond. ed.) 167, (235) says, that Dr. Arnold's chapter on the laws of the twelve tables is one of the most valuable, if not the most so, in the whole history.

70. The laws of the twelve tables are referred to by the jurisconsults, and in the constitutions of the emperors, as the *jus vetus*, *jus priscum*, *leges veteres*, *lex antiqua*, *jus antiquissimum*, and sometimes as the *jus civile*, *jus decemvirale*.[1]

Section II. — *Laws made by the People.*

71. After the establishment of the laws of the twelve tables, no other act of general legislation took place until the time of Justinian. But, during the republic, and for some short period afterwards, laws were made, from time to time, as occasion required, by the people, in their assemblies. These laws were of two kinds, namely, laws properly so called, and plebiscites; which differed rather in the mode of their enactment, than in their authority. The former, being first agreed upon or decreed by the senate, were then proposed by a magistrate of senatorial dignity, to the Roman people, and were accepted or rejected by their suffrages. The latter were enacted by the commonalty (*plebs*) only, upon the proposition of a plebeian magistrate. The word commonalty (*plebs*), says Justinian, differs from people (*populus*), as a species differs from its genus; for

---

[1] A general statement of the contents of the twelve tables is given by Chancellor Kent, in a note to the last lecture, in the first volume of his Commentaries.

all the citizens, including patricians and senators, are comprehended under the term people; while the term commonalty only includes all the citizens except patricians and senators.[1] Laws of the first kind were properly denominated *leges*, and also *populiscita*, as being made by the whole people; those of the latter description were called *plebiscita*, as being made by the plebeians only. The plebiscites, by a change in the original constitution of the republic, which took place about the year 300 of Rome, acquired the force and authority of law.

72. The laws enacted by the people were proposed to them in the form in which they were to be received or rejected, and were not discussed or amended, but simply voted upon. The mode of proceeding seems to have been precisely similar to what takes place in most of the states, in amending the constitution; the amendment being prepared beforehand by the legislature or by a convention called for the purpose, and then submitted to the votes of the people. A law, thus proposed, was called a *rogatio*, from the verb *rogo;* and, sometimes, but improperly, retained the same appellation after it had been agreed to; precisely as we sometimes use the word *bill*, in speaking of a law which has passed.

73. The terms, relative to legislation, are thus explained by Ulpian: "A *lex* is said either *rogari* or *ferri;* it is said *abrogari*, when it is repealed; it is

---

[1] Inst. I. 2, 4.

said *derogari*, when a part is repealed; it is said *subrogari*, when some addition is made to it; and it is said *obrogari*, when some part of it is changed."[1]

74. These laws, so far as relates to their form, were generally comprised in a single paragraph, and had but a single object in view. They were sometimes, however, divided into chapters; and, towards the end of the republic, several laws were adopted, which embraced a number of distinct topics.

75. The title of a law was generally derived from the name of the magistrate who proposed it, as the law *Hortensia*, from the dictator Hortensius. Sometimes the name was taken from the two consuls or other magistrates, as the *lex Acilia Calpurnia*, *Ælia* or *Ælia Sentia*, *Papia* or *Papia Poppæa*, and others. Sometimes a law received its designation from its object, as the *lex Cincia de Donis et Muneribus*, the *lex Furia Testamentaria*, the *lex Julia Municipalis*. Where several laws related to a common object, they were often designated by a collective name, as the *leges Agrariæ*, *Judiciariæ*, and others. Where a law consisted of several chapters, a particular chapter was sometimes referred to by the title of the law, with the addition of a reference to the contents of the chapter, as, for example, the *lex Julia de Fundo Dotali*, which was a chapter of the *lex Julia de Adulteriis*. A law sometimes took its name from its principal subject, or from its first chapter, as the

---

[1] Frag. I. 3.

lex Julia de maritandis Ordinibus. Sometimes a law comprised various provisions relating to matters essentially different, and, in that case, it was called *lex Satura.* This mode of legislation was at length forbidden, by the *lex Cæcilia Didia,* on the ground that the people might thereby be compelled either to vote for something which they did not approve, or to reject something which they did approve, if it was proposed to them in this manner.[1]

76. This form of legislation continued in use for some time after the destruction of the republic; and various laws are mentioned as having been passed under the empire, such as the *lex Junia,* under Tibe-

---

[1] There is nothing in the rules of parliamentary practice, in the legislative assemblies of modern times, to prevent the including of subjects essentially different in the same bill or act. It seems to have been usual, at one time, in the British parliament, at the end of a session, to throw a number of miscellaneous articles into the same bill, which, on that account, was called a *hotchpot* bill. Parl. Reg. vii. 275. When one of the branches of a legislative assembly passes a bill, which the other branch has no authority to amend, but only to accept or reject, and sends such bill to the latter, with other provisions included in it, which are distasteful to that branch, but which it must agree to or lose the whole bill, this is called *tacking*, and is extremely unparliamentary. Thus, in the British parliament, where the house of commons is alone authorized to grant supplies, without any interference on the part of the lords, who can only accept or reject, but not amend a bill for that purpose, if the house of commons should send up a bill of supply, with enactments included in it which the lords would reject, if they were embraced in a separate bill, and thus attempt to compel the lords to agree to the latter, at the risk of losing the whole bill, such a proceeding would be deemed a great infringement of the privileges of the lords. May's Law, &c. of Parliament, 409.

rius; soon after which, the power of making laws was taken from the people, and given exclusively to the senate. Numerous enactments of this description took place under Julius and Augustus Cæsar, which are known by the general name of the *leges Juliæ*, or the Julian laws.

77. A list of the principal laws made by the people, amounting to about three hundred in number, is given by Smith, in his Dictionary of Greek and Roman Antiquities.[1] These laws, so far as we can judge of them by the fragments which remain, though the terms, in which they were expressed, were fixed by the persons who proposed them, were carefully drawn, both as to matter and language. The author just referred to says, that "The Romans seem to have always adhered to the old expressions, and to have used few superfluous words. Great care was taken with such clauses as were proposed to alter a former law; and great care was also used to avoid all interference with a former law, when no change in it was intended."[2]

---

[1] Dictionary of Greek and Roman Antiquities, edited by William Smith, LL. D. Boston and London, 1849. The articles on the Roman law, of which the work contains a great number, were written by George Long, Esq., from whose Discourses I have inserted a quotation in a preceding note, *ante*, 47. The list of laws is given under the word *Lex*, and commences on page 684.

[2] Ib. 682.

Section III. — *Laws made by the Senate.*

78. A law enacted by the senate of Rome was denominated a *senatus-consultum.* Acts of this description, during the republic, had not the force of laws, except in certain particular cases, unless they were approved by the people, as already mentioned under the head of laws enacted by the people. In the time of Augustus, the *senatus-consulta* began to take the place of the *leges*, properly so called; and, when the assemblies of the people, without which a proper *lex* could not be enacted, were abolished under the emperors, the *senatus-consulta* became an accustomed form of legislation, and so continued until superseded by the imperial constitutions.

79. The *senatus-consulta* were passed upon the proposition of the emperor, made by him to the senate, in the form of a law; and when the senate had approved the proposition, which was always done, as a matter of course, a decree was rendered accordingly, which became the law. It was thus that the earlier Roman emperors, by leaving the people and the senate in possession of the semblance of power, respected the forms of the republic, after they had in fact seized upon the whole power of the state.

80. It seems, that, after the accession of Augustus, the senate and people conferred various honors and powers upon him, at different times. In the year 724, of the city, they made him tribune for life. In

727, they exempted him from the coercion of the laws. In 731, he was created perpetual consul; and in 735, a power was given to him either of amending or making whatever laws he thought proper. These and other decrees, originally rendered in favor of Augustus, were afterwards generally renewed at the commencement of the reign of every new emperor; and, by being frequently renewed together, became, as it were, one law, and were called *Lex Imperii*, or *Regia*.

81. The existence of such a law, though stated explicitly by Ulpian, in the Digest,[1] had been frequently doubted. The language attributed to Ulpian is, that, by this law, all the power which had formerly belonged to the people became transferred to the emperor. Those who entertained doubts supposed that this passage had been interpolated by Justinian, for the purpose of giving a legal color to his own enactments. But this, and many other obscure and doubtful points in the Roman law, were entirely cleared up by the newly-discovered commentaries or institutes of Gaius, one of the jurists, whose writings were made use of by Justinian in his compilation. This author corroborates Ulpian, and settles the question of the existence of the *Lex Regia*, as a fundamental law of the Roman Empire.

82. It does not appear that the emperors exercised at once, and to its full extent, the power con-

---

[1] Book I. Tit. 4.

ferred on them by the royal laws; but as the people became accustomed to the exercise of this power, the emperors gradually dispensed with the ancient forms, and exercised a legislative function, abrogating the ancient laws, and making new ones, of their own authority, and without even the ceremony of consulting the senate. The usage of *senatus-consulta*, however, did not entirely cease until the reign of Antoninus Caracalla.

83. The *senatus-consulta* were designated sometimes by the name of the consuls, as *Silanianum* from Silanus, *Libonianum* from Libo, *Memmianum* from Memmius; sometimes from the name of the emperor, as *Claudianum* from Claudius, *Neronianum* from Nero; sometimes from the subject-matter, as *de Bacchanalibus;* sometimes from the name of the consul or emperor, with the addition of the subject-matter, as *Neronianum de Legatis;* sometimes they are designated as made *auctore* or *auctoritate Hadriani*, &c. The *senatus-consultum Macedonianum*, which provided that a loan of money to a son of a family should be void, even after the death of his father, took its name from Macedo, a notorious usurer, to whose practices it alluded.

84. A *senatus-consultum*, of the time of the emperor Adrian, relating to the *petitio hæreditatis*, is preserved entire, with all the formal parts, in the Digest,[1] but it bears no name. The terms of the *senatus-*

---

[1] Book V. Tit. 3, 20.

consultum Macedonianum are also preserved in the Digest.[1] The following is a somewhat free translation of this *senatus-consultum*, which forms the subject of the whole title, in which it occurs:—"Whereas among the different crimes of which Macedo was guilty, was that of extortion, and whereas, by lending money to sons of a family he furnished them with the means of debauchery, to the great depravation of morals; therefore, it is decreed, that he who lends money to the son of a family shall not have any action to recover the same, even after the death of the father; in order that those who lend money may know, that, by reason of the bad example which they give in this respect, the obligation thereby contracted can never become legally binding, and that they need not expect to add any thing to the validity of their claims by the death of the father."

85. The laws passed by the emperors, under the name of *senatus-consulta*, appear to have related chiefly to matters of private right; all constitutional changes, which were frequently the subject of the *leges*, properly so called, being entirely, or in a great degree, superseded by the royal laws already alluded to.

---

[1] Book XIV. Tit. 6.

SECTION IV.—*Imperial Constitutions.*

86. The emperors exercised the powers with which they were invested by the royal law, by means of what were called constitutions. An imperial constitution, in the broadest sense of the term, embraced every instrument by which the head of the state declared his pleasure, either in a matter of legislation, administration, or jurisdiction.

87. These constitutions were of different kinds, and received their designation, according to the nature and subject-matter of their provisions. A *decretum* was a judgment in a matter in dispute between two parties, brought before the emperor, either in the way of appeal, or in the first instance. *Edicta*, so called from analogy to the old edicts, which will be described hereafter, were laws binding on all the emperor's subjects. Under the general head of *rescripta* were contained *epistolæ* and *subscriptiones*, which were the answers of the emperor to those who consulted him, either as public functionaries, or as individuals. Constitutions, which in their nature, were limited to special cases, were not considered as general laws.

88. The number of imperial constitutions of all these different kinds, which were promulgated by the emperors, is almost infinite. Four collections of them have been made, the Gregorian, the Hermo-

genian, the Theodosian, and that of Justinian; to all of which, the term *codex*, or code, is applied.

89. The Gregorian code, which included the constitutions of the emperors, from the time of Adrian to that of Diocletian and Maximian, is supposed to have been the work of a private individual, though it was received as authority in courts of justice. The author is not known with certainty, but the work is attributed to Gregorius, who was prefect of the prætor, in the time of Constantine the great. This code consisted of thirteen books, at least, which were divided into titles.

90. The Hermogenian code was probably a mere supplement of the former, contained in one book. The two are usually referred to as one work.

91. The Theodosian code was compiled by the directions of the emperor Theodosius the younger; who, in the year 429 of the Christian era, appointed a commission, consisting of eight persons, to form into a code all the edicts and *leges generales*, from the time of Constantine, according to the model of the Gregorian and Hermogenian code. This code was completed, and promulgated as law, in the year 438, for both the eastern and western empire, and was declared to be a substitute for all the constitutions made since the time of Constantine. The Theodosian code consists of sixteen books, the greater part of which, as well as the subsequent constitutions of Theodosius, exist at the present day in their genuine

state. The books are divided into titles, and the titles are subdivided into sections or laws.[1]

92. The code of Justinian, which contained the fourth collection of imperial constitutions, compiled from all the preceding codes and constitutions then existing, makes a part of the great legal reform of that emperor, and will be described when that branch of the subject is treated of.

93. A considerable number of these constitutions is preserved in their original form, in the extant codes. The preface to the Institutes is a constitution *de Confirmatione Institutionum.*

94. To recapitulate, briefly, the history of Roman Legislation, from the earliest times to that of Justinian :—1. The Laws of the Twelve Tables, which were compiled and promulgated about the year 300 of Rome, or 450 years before the Christian era; 2. *Leges,* properly so called, made by the people, either with or without the concurrence of the senate, from the time of the establishment of the twelve tables, during the whole period of the republic, that is, to the year 726 of Rome, or twenty-seven years before the Christian era, and for some short time after the accession of Augustus ; 3. *Senatus-consulta,* which, in form only, were the acts of the senate, but in reality were dictated by the

---

[1] This code was edited and published by J. Godfrey, or Gothofredus, in 1635, reëdited by Ritter, and published between 1736 and 1745, in six volumes folio.

emperors, from the accession of Augustus, to the time of Caracalla, who succeeded to the empire in the year 212 of the Christian era; and, 4. Imperial Constitutions, commencing a long time before the disuse of *senatus-consulta*, and continued to the time of Justinian, and afterwards to the end of the empire.

CHAPTER IV.

HISTORY OF ROMAN JURISPRUDENCE ANTERIOR TO THE TIME OF JUSTINIAN.

95. THE several branches of the Roman law, which have just been considered under the head of Legislation, constituted the framework, as it were, of the vast structure of Roman Jurisprudence, which will be treated of in the present chapter. But, before proceeding, it will be useful to take notice of an important difference between the legal polity of the states of antiquity, and that to which we are accustomed. In modern times, and especially in this country, the distinction between the legislative and judicial powers is strongly marked, and the functions of the two are carefully separated. Ample provision is made, too, for the regular exercise of the former, as well as the latter. Legislative bodies are in the stated and frequent, if not in the constant, exercise of their official powers, and ready to supply all the demands made by the wants of the people for new legislation.

96. It appears to have been quite otherwise among the nations of antiquity. In Rome, the ad-

ministration of justice was abundantly provided for. But the making or revising of laws, properly so called, at least during the time of the republic, was only an occasional thing. New laws might indeed be made, and were in fact made, in the manner already described. But the power was rarely exercised, and when exercised, chiefly for political or constitutional purposes.

97. The consequence was, that in ancient Rome, much that would have been referred in modern times to the legislative power, was left to the judicial. Hence, as will be seen, the invention of forms of action, and of certain fictions, by means of which the letter of the law was respected, while its deficiencies were supplied, or its strictness moderated and tempered. The principle seems to have been fully recognized, that it was an indispensable necessity, that justice should be administered, at all events; conformably to the law, and in pursuance of its provisions, if there was any law applicable to the case; but if the law was silent, or inadequate, or obsolete, still justice was to be done; and the mode of doing it was left to the ingenuity and skill of the jurisconsults, and the ultimate sanction of the tribunals.

98. Jurisprudence can never, under any circumstances, be entirely superseded by legislation, however particular and minute the latter may be;[1] and

---

[1] See *ante*, 33, 34.

even where the legislative body is in the full and almost constant exercise of its functions, as with us, the necessity of jurisprudence is as great and as absolute as it was in ancient Rome. No statute can ever be passed, which will not give rise to questions, that must be settled by a reference to something besides its own terms. But the occasion for jurisprudence is not so frequent, comparatively speaking, at the present time, nor is its province so extensive, as among the nations of antiquity.

99. The establishment of the principles, which are evolved in the application of the law to particular cases, ordinarily takes place, at least in modern times, by means of the tribunals of justice. But this is by no means essential. In whatever manner the application of the law is made, or remedial justice administered, whether by the agency of courts of justice, by the advice of learned men, or by the customs and usages of the people, the principles thus developed are equally obligatory, and as much constitute jurisprudence, as if they emanated from a judicial tribunal. Under this head, therefore, are to be included every mode or form of proceeding, every institution, and every custom or usage which had for its object, or was in fact connected with, the application of the law in the practical administration of justice.

100. It is proposed now to take a survey of the Roman Jurisprudence, anterior to the time of Justinian, under the several heads following: 1. Sym-

bolical Acts; 2. Actions of the Law; 3 Formulas; 4. Prætorian or honorary law; 5. Jurisconsults and *Jus Respondendi;* 6. Rival Sects or Schools; 7. Law of Citation; and, 8. Imperial Rescripts and Decrees.

Section I. — *Symbolical Acts.*

101. At the period of the enactment of the laws of the twelve tables, important proceedings, affecting the legal rights and relations of the citizens, took place, and the knowledge of them was preserved and perpetuated, by means of symbolical acts. This appears to have resulted, in part, from the intimate connection which then subsisted between the rites and ceremonies of religion, and the daily habits and business of the people, and in part from the fact, that such symbolical acts furnished an obvious mode of perpetuating the memory of events, which is now effected by means of writing and records.

102. Legal acts, that is, acts which effected, or were intended to effect, changes in the legal relations of individuals, either took place or were accompanied by ceremonies more or less significant of the events or acts to which they referred. Thus, for example, the contract of pledge was said to be formed by closing the hand; that of mandate, by giving the right hand; the acceptance of an inheritance by the heir was signified by his snapping his

fingers;[1] the prescription or limitation resulting from adverse possession was interrupted by breaking a branch of a tree; when one wished to make an objection, in legal form, to the continuation of a work which might be injurious to him, he did so by casting a small stone.

103. These symbolical acts, which were undoubtedly in use at the time of the enactment of the twelve tables, were not the object of any particular legislation, and in fact none was necessary; they made a part of the habits and customs of the people, the existence of which is always presupposed by every system of law. Symbolical acts of this kind have been in use in times much more recent. The ceremony of livery of seisin, and of continual claim, besides others in the common law, are examples. Some of these acts were required to be performed in the presence of a magistrate, as adoption and emancipation; others, as the alienation of land, had no need of his presence.

104. It was necessary that every legal act should strictly follow the solemn forms, and be expressed in the prescribed terms; otherwise the proceeding would be null and void. It is said, that the jurisconsults, who were all of the patrician order, made use of the superstitious veneration in which these

---

[1] Gibbon also adds, that the heir was sometimes obliged to cast away his garments, and to leap and dance with real or affected transport. But this is said by his German commentator to be *absolutely false*. See Gibbon's History, Milman's Ed. V. 181, (247) n. 50.

forms and ceremonies were held by the people, in order to keep them in dependence; and that it was for this purpose that they invented those different rites and combinations of words, which were equally complicated and inviolable, and applied them not only to acts which were necessary to be passed in the presence of a magistrate, but even to the greater number of those in which his presence was not necessary.

105. The ceremony attending the emancipation of a son from the paternal power, which was performed by turning him round with a gentle blow on the cheek, affords a good illustration of the nature and effect of those symbolic acts, which were performed in the presence of a magistrate, as well as of the fictitious proceedings, which were resorted to and sanctioned for the furtherance of justice. It was a principle of policy among the ancient Romans, that the paternal power could not be dissolved in such a manner as to make the son *sui juris*, that is, competent himself to become the head of a family. But it was established also by law, that the father might sell his son, and thus transfer the paternal power over him to another person. At the same time, in order to prevent the dissolution of the paternal power, the law also provided, that if the purchaser should attempt to give the son his freedom by emancipating him, the son should instantly fall back into the power of the father, and be in the same state in which he was before the sale. The father might then sell him again.

106. Such appears to have been the law before and at the time of the enactment of the laws of the twelve tables. According to these laws, the father still retained the power of selling his children, and even of putting them to death. The twelve tables also provided, that if a father sold his son three times, the son should not fall back into the power of the father, if the third purchaser manumitted him. This was the foundation of an invention of the jurisconsults, by means of which the principle already mentioned was completely abrogated in point of fact, while it was apparently respected; and a father was enabled to dissolve the paternal power and make his son a free man. This was effected by going through with the ceremony of three pretended sales and three emancipations, after which the son, according to the laws of the twelve tables, became *sui juris.*

107. This fictitious proceeding was doubtless sanctioned, because the public sentiment had got the start of positive legislation, and demanded an abrogation of the ancient law in certain cases. It does not seem to have occurred to anybody, that the whole thing was really a sham; but it does not become even us to reproach the Romans with the use of fictions; whilst plaintiffs, in our courts of justice, are every day gravely informing the court, that they have casually lost divers and sundry commodities, of which they never even had possession.

SECTION II.—*Actions of the Law.*

108. The laws of the twelve tables, though engraved on brass and set up in a public place, in order that every one might know his rights and their extent, did not point out in what manner those rights were to be exercised, either in bringing or in defending against an action. The jurisconsults, therefore, invented solemn forms of proceeding, which were called *actions of the law*, either because their function was to put the laws in execution, or because they were strictly adapted to the words of the law and could not be varied.

109. According to Gaius, there were five modes of proceeding, denominated actions of the law:—1. *Sacramento;* 2. *Per Judicis Postulationem;* 3. *Per Condictionem;* 4. *Per Manus Injectionem;* 5. *Per Pignoris Captionem.* These proceedings did not commence, of course, until the parties had made their appearance before the magistrate.

110. I. The first of these modes was generally adopted, like the modern action of the case, where no other specific form had been prescribed by law. In this proceeding, when the parties were before the magistrate, each of them staked a certain sum of money, *sacramentum*, on the issue of their suit; five hundred asses, if the value of the disputed property amounted to one thousand asses or more; or fifty, if it fell below that sum. If the suit related to the

freedom of one claimed as a slave, the *sacramentum* was fixed in favor of liberty at the lower sum of fifty asses. The party who lost his cause lost also the money staked, which went into the public treasury.

111. The magistrate, thereupon, appointed a *judex*[1]

---

[1] The functions of the *Judex*, according to the system of Roman procedure, appear to have been nearly the same with those of jurors in modern times. The magistrate, before whom an action was brought or a complaint instituted, did not generally investigate the facts in dispute, but for this purpose appointed a judex and gave him the necessary instructions. When the judex was appointed, the proceedings before the prætor were terminated. The parties then appeared before the judex and proceeded to trial, upon evidence and the hearing of their respective advocates, as in modern times. The judex was at liberty, if necessary, to avail himself of the aid of the legal advice of the jurisconsults, who were then said in *consilio adesse*, but the judex alone was empowered to give judgment. In many, perhaps most, cases, a single judex was appointed; in others, and especially in criminal cases, several were appointed, who were sometimes called *Recuperatores*. Where several were appointed, they voted by ballot, and a majority determined the verdict; if the votes were equal there was an acquittal. The instructions received beforehand by the judex from the magistrate were probably nothing more than a commission to try the cause, containing only very general directions, if any, in matters of law. In exercising the authority to advise with the jurisconsults, upon the law, in the course of the trial, they had recourse to a legitimate source of information; the jurisconsults being authorized expounders of the law. An authority, somewhat similar, was given to jurors in Massachusetts, by a law of the colony, which provided as follows: "It is further ordered, that whenever any jury or jurors are not clear in their judgments or conscience, concerning any case wherein they are to give their verdict, they shall have liberty in open court (but not otherwise) to advise with any man they shall think fit to resolve or direct them, before they give in their verdict." Ancient Charters and Laws of Massachusetts Bay, 145.

to try the cause, before whom the parties appeared, and briefly stated the nature of their respective claims. Then, the object in dispute, if it was a living thing, or susceptible of being moved, was brought into court, and the plaintiff, holding a rod or wand in one hand, and laying hold of the thing in dispute with the other, asserted that it belonged to him according to law, and laid his rod upon it. The other party did the same, and asserted his right in a similar manner. They were then directed by the judex to loose their hold of the thing; which being done, the plaintiff turned to the defendant and requested to be told by him, wherefore he had claimed the thing in question as his own. The defendant answered, that he had done all that the law required of him, by making his claim in the manner he had done. Then the plaintiff replied, that as the defendant had made a wrongful claim, he defied him at law, and staked five hundred asses on the issue, to which the defendant rejoined, that in like manner and with a like stake he defied the plaintiff.

112. The judex then directed that possession of the thing in dispute should be taken by one of the parties, until the cause should be decided, upon his giving proper security to his adversary, *litis et vindiciarum*, that is, that he would make good to him both the thing itself, *litem*, and the benefit arising from the temporary possession of it, *vindicias*, if the cause should be finally decided against him. Both

parties at the same time gave security to the judex that the money staked, the *sacramentum*, should be duly paid. If the dispute related to the personal freedom of any man,—that is, whether he should be adjudged to be a slave or a freeman,—the twelve tables provided that the temporary possession should be awarded in favor of freedom, or, in other words, that the man should remain at liberty till it was proved that he was lawfully a slave.

113. II. III. The commentaries of Gaius, to which we are indebted for all that is now known with certainty relative to the actions of the law, have not been restored at the particular part where the second and third forms are described. The second, *per postulationem judicis*, was an application to the magistrate to appoint a judex to try the matter in dispute. The third, the *actio per condictionem*, from what little is said by Gaius, appears to have been a sort of notice to the adverse party, calling on him to appear at the end of thirty days, to submit his cause to the judge.

114. IV. The fourth form of proceeding, *per manus injectionem*, was allowed by the twelve tables as a method of enforcing the fulfilment of the sentence rendered by the judex. If the defendant, after having lost his cause and been sentenced to pay a certain sum to the plaintiff, neglected for thirty days to pay according to the sentence, the plaintiff was allowed to lay actual hands on him, and unless he

could find a *vindex*,[1] or defender, to represent and defend him, he himself not being allowed to resist, the defendant was dragged to the plaintiff's house and there kept in chains till he had paid all that was due.

115. V. The last form of proceeding, the action *per pignoris captionem*, was a sort of distress, by means of which a party was allowed, in certain cases, to compel his debtor to make payment, by carrying off articles of the debtor's property as a pledge. According to an ancient custom, a soldier, if his pay was withheld, was allowed to distrain in this manner upon the goods of the officer, whose business it was to give it to him. The twelve tables extended the same remedy to other cases connected with religious worship; as, for instance, it was permitted against one who had bought a beast for sacrifice and had not paid for it.

116. The forms of legal proceedings seem to have been made use of by the patricians, for the purpose of maintaining the ascendency and advancing the interests of their order, at the expense of the plebeians. These forms, being most intimately connected with the religious rites and ceremonies of the people, were regarded with equal veneration; they were known only to persons of the patrician rank, who filled all the offices both of the magistracy and of the priesthood, and performed also the functions

---

1 See *ante*, 68, note.

of jurisconsults; the forms of proceeding were required to be observed with the greatest particularity, and on certain fixed days; and thus the plebeians, whenever they had occasion to be informed of their legal rights, or to prosecute or defend them, by actions or other proceedings at law, being themselves wholly ignorant both of the proper forms and times, were necessarily obliged to apply to the patricians for their aid.

117. An example of the excessive refinement and nicety with which the actions of the law were conducted, which is mentioned by Gaius, is well worthy of the ingenuity of our own times. By the laws of the twelve tables it was forbidden to cut down fruit trees, generally, without specifying any one kind in particular. A plaintiff, who had brought his action for an injury to his vines, was nonsuited, on the ground that he did not bring his case within the law, which related to trees and not to vines; though it was admitted, that he could have maintained his action, by the proof of an injury to his vines, provided he had described it as an injury to his fruit trees.

118. The same strictness of proceeding being requisite, as we have already seen, in relation to legal acts which were not required to be done before the magistrate, and the knowledge of the forms being also exclusively in the hands of the patricians, the dependence of the plebeians upon them seems to have been complete. The former could not accept

a succession, contract an engagement, renounce a property, or grant an estate, go to law, or defend themselves against an action, without using these sacred forms, that is to say, without the aid of a jurisconsult.

119. It is not, therefore, to be wondered at, that the patricians, deriving such an advantage from their exclusive knowledge of the forms of actions, should have been at great pains to conceal them from the people. It was a rule, that the forms should be observed by the parties themselves, and that they could not be done by others acting for them. Hence a party could not dispense with a knowledge of the forms himself, as one may do at the present day, by employing an attorney, but was obliged to perform them in his own person; and, on the other hand, if he knew the forms he would have no occasion to resort to the jurisconsults for aid.

120. The code of forms, for all these proceedings, was accordingly preserved with the greatest care, in the possession of the patrician pontiffs, who were thus the oracles both of divine and human laws. But their precautions were at length defeated for a time. In the year 449 of Rome, the book of forms was copied by Flavius, who was the secretary of one of the pontiffs, and published for the use of the people; a service for which the people were so grateful, that they made Flavius an edile, although he was a person of a mean condition, being the son of a freedman. The collection thus published was

called the *Flavian Law.* It was considered as a source of law second only to the twelve tables, the former being the practice, while the latter was the theory.

121. After the publication of the Flavian Law new actions were invented for the new cases that occurred, which were published by Ælius Sextus, in a collection made by him, containing: 1. The text of the laws of the twelve tables; 2. Their interpretation; 3. The ancient actions of the law, together with those which had been newly framed. This collection was known by the name of the *Ælian Law.* The *actiones legis* were abolished on account of their excessive nicety, which continued the same after their publication as before, by the *lex Æbutia*, which is of uncertain date, and by two of the *leges Juliæ*, about the 728th year of Rome.

Section III. — *Formulas.*

122. After the abolition of the actions of the law, a system of procedure became established, which dispensed with the symbolic acts, and was conducted by means of the *formulas* alone, which were a part of the ancient procedure. The invention of the formulas, which superseded the actions of the law, is attributed to the prætors, who were the principal magistrates concerned in the administration of justice, and whose functions will be explained under the head of the prætorian or honorary law.

123. These formulas were the statements made by the parties, in the presence of the magistrate, in the prosecution and defence of actions. It has already been seen, from the laws of the twelve tables, in what manner the parties came or were brought before the tribunal. The plaintiff had no occasion to use any formula, written or verbal, to compel his adversary to appear; no writ was necessary, as in modern times; the plaintiff's assertion was sufficient, in the first instance; and if the defendant did not comply with his request to appear, the plaintiff called witnesses, and thereupon dragged his adversary before the magistrate.

124. When the parties were before the magistrate the affair proceeded by the use of the formulas, of which a short general description only will be necessary in this place.

125. The formula consisted of four parts, the *demonstratio*, *intentio*, *adjudicatio*, *condemnatio*. The *demonstratio* was that part which explained what was the subject-matter of the action. The *intentio* stated the claim of the plaintiff. The *adjudicatio* was that part which gave the judex authority to adjudge the thing in dispute to one or the other of the litigant parties. The *condemnatio* was that part of the formula which gave the judex authority to condemn the defendant in a sum of money, or to acquit him. These four parts could not all occur in the same proceeding; because, if it contained the *adjudicatio*, it could not also contain the *condemnatio*, the one being a substitute for the other, according

to the nature of the claim. Sometimes the *intentio* alone was requisite, as, for example, in those proceedings which were denominated *prejudiciales*, in which the matter for inquiry was, whether a certain fact existed, as, for instance, whether a certain person was a freedman or not.

126. The formula also contained what we are accustomed to denominate the pleadings, that is to say, the statements and counter statements of the plaintiff and the defendant. The *intentio* was the declaration. If this was met by an *exceptio*, or plea, on the part of the defendant, the latter was also inserted in the formula. Then came the *replicatio*, and subsequent pleadings. In conclusion, the formula contained directions for the judex, and gave him power to act in the matter.

127. The formulas were deemed of so great importance, and so much weight was attributed to them, in the commencement of actions, and in the rendition of judgments, that every thing in fact depended upon their being properly observed; so that, notwithstanding the abolition of the old actions of the law, legal proceedings were still conducted with extreme subtlety and refinement. If the least formality was neglected, on the part of the plaintiff, he failed altogether in his suit; if the neglect was on the part of the judex, he thereby rendered himself a party to the suit, and became himself liable to condemnation.

128. The formulas remained in use until the reign

of Diocletian; when the mode of rendering justice was entirely changed, and the proceedings were from thenceforth conducted more according to principles of equity, than to established forms.

129. At a later period, when Constantine had established several new magistracies, and changed the constitution of the state, the old method of proceeding became entirely useless; so that when Justinian came to make his revision, he made no mention whatever of the ancient forms of actions, and treated the general subject so slightly, that, until within a few years, there was very little to be known with certainty, relative to the forms of legal proceedings. The matter has been, to a great extent, elucidated by the discovery of the commentaries of Gaius, in the year 1816; but still there are many points which remain to be cleared up. The subject of procedure among the Romans, is rather curious than useful; though some knowledge of it is needful, in order to understand the peculiar meaning of many terms which are constantly occurring in the texts of the law; precisely, as one would be at a loss to understand a great many terms and expressions in the older English reports, without some knowledge of ancient forms of proceeding, which have long since become obsolete.

Section IV. — *Prætorian or Honorary Law.*

130. This important branch of the Roman law derives its name from the *prætor*, who was the magistrate chiefly concerned with the administration of justice. The office of prætor was first established in the year 587 of Rome, on the suggestion of the patricians. The reason assigned was, that the consuls were frequently absent in command of the armies of the republic, and it was necessary that there should be an officer appointed to take their place, and administer justice, during their absence. The new officer was taken from the patrician order, as a sort of indemnification for their having been obliged to share the consulship with the plebeians. And it was thirty years, or more, before any plebeian was appointed to the office.

131. The chief function of the prætor, and the only one, with which we have any concern, was to administer justice. Some years afterwards, another prætor was appointed, whose business it was to administer justice between strangers, who happened to be in Rome, or between strangers and Roman citizens; and who was accordingly denominated the *strangers'* prætor. The other prætor was then called the *prætor urbanus, qui jus inter cives dicit*, or simply *prætor urbanus*, or *prætor urbis*. The two prætors determined by lot which functions they should respectively exercise. The number of prætors was occasionally increased. The office was annual.

132. It has already been more than once stated, that, whilst the power of direct legislation was only occasionally called into exercise, the judicial power was always active, always accessible to the citizen, and always in the exercise of its proper functions. Justice was to be administered, and it was the business of the magistrate to see that it was done. If the existing law afforded the means of doing justice, the law was applied. If the law was deficient, it was the business of the magistrate to supply all deficiencies. Hence, it was an established power of all the higher magistrates to make edicts. This power, the *jus edicendi*, was principally exercised by the two prætors, already described, the city prætor and the strangers' prætor.

133. The edict may be described in general terms, as a rule promulgated by a magistrate on entering on the duties of his office, by writing it on an album, and placing it in a conspicuous place. In this way the prætors were accustomed to announce beforehand, in what manner, and by what rules, they should administer justice, during the year for which they were appointed. If it was the business of these magistrates to administer justice only according to and within the strict terms of the positive law, it is clear that an edict, merely announcing that fact, would be an idle ceremony. Hence, it is manifest, that the magistrate had some further function to perform, which it was his duty to explain beforehand by means of his edict. It can scarcely be doubted, that

the rules thus promulgated were those principles of jurisprudence which had already been developed in the administration of justice, and by the usage of the people, with such additions as the experience of each prætor might suggest to him as useful and proper.

134. As the office of a magistrate was only annual, the rules promulgated by one could not be binding on his successor; though the latter might confirm or adopt them, and introduce them into his own edict. Such adopted rules were known as the *edictum tralatitium*, or *vetus*, as opposed to the *edictum novum*. The edict, usually given by a magistrate, was intended to apply to all cases to which it might be applicable, during the year of his office; and hence it was sometimes called the *lex annua*. It was in his power, however, to make an edict at any time during his term of office, for a particular occasion.

135. Each prætor generally adopting the edict of his predecessor, with the addition of something of his own, the edicts soon constituted, in fact, a large body of law, which was practically of as much importance as any other part of the law. The several edicts, when thus established, were designated by the names of their promulgators, as the *edictum Carbonianum;* or they were named with reference to the formula, and the action which they established, as *Publiciana*, &c.

136. The origin of the power of making an edict

cannot be shown historically, but as the prætor was appointed to supply the place of the consuls, in the administration of justice, and the consular power was the representation of the kingly power, it seems not unreasonable to suppose, that the *jus edicendi* may have been coeval with the latter. But whatever its origin, it was very early exercised, and at, or perhaps somewhat previous to, the time of Cicero, the *jus prætorium* was a recognized part, forming already a large division, of law.

137. The prætorian law was not only admitted in usage, but it was recognized and regulated by a law of the people. In the year 686 of Rome, it was provided by the *lex Cornelia*, (a plebiscite,) that the prætor, in the decision of particular cases, occurring during his term of office, should conform to the edict published by him at the commencement of his year. It appears, that in the time of Cicero, the edict had become so considerable a body of law, that an attempt was then made to reduce it into order, and to comment upon it.

138. The following summary, taken from a work already referred to,[1] will serve to give a general description of the character and object of this important branch of the Roman jurisprudence.

139. "The object of the edict, according to the Roman jurists, was the following: '*Adjuvandi vel supplendi vel corrigendi juris civilis gratia propter*

---

[1] Smith's Dictionary of Greek and Roman Antiquities, 445.

utilitatem publicam': the edict is also described as '*viva vox juris civilis.*' It was, in effect, an indirect method of legislating, and it was the means by which numerous rules of law became established. It was found to be a more effectual, because an easier and more practical, way of gradually enlarging and altering the existing law, and keeping the whole system in harmony, than the method of direct legislation; and it is undeniable, that the most valuable part of the Roman law is derived from the edicts."

140. "If a prætor established any rule which was found to be inconvenient or injurious, it fell into disuse, if not adopted by his successor. The publicity of the edict must also have been a great security against any arbitrary changes, for a *magistratus* would hardly venture to promulgate a rule to which opinion had not, by anticipation, already given its sanction. Many of the rules promulgated by the edict were merely in conformity to existing custom, more particularly in cases of contracts, and thus the edict would have the effect of converting custom into law. This is what Cicero seems to mean (*de Invent.* ii. 22,) when he says that the edict depends, in a great degree, on custom."

141. "As to the matter of the edict, it must be supposed, that the defects of the existing law must generally have been acknowledged and felt, before any *magistratus* ventured to supply them; and, in doing this, he must have conformed to the so-called

equity, *jus naturale* or *gentium*. Under the emperors, also, it may be presumed, that the opinions of legal writers would act on public opinion, and on those who had the *jus edicendi*. Hence, a large part of the edictal rules were founded on the so called *jus gentium;* and the necessity of some modifications of the strict rules of the civil law, and of additional rules of law, would become the more apparent with the extension of the Roman power, and their intercourse with other nations."

142. "But the method in which the prætor introduced new rules of law, was altogether conformable to the spirit of Roman institutions. The process was slow and gradual; it was not effected by the destruction of that which existed, but by adapting it to circumstances. Accordingly, when a right existed, or was recognized, the prætor would give an action, if there was none; he would interfere by way of protecting possession, but he could not make possession into ownership, and, accordingly, that was effected by the law; he aided plaintiffs by fictions, as, for instance, in the *Publiciana actio*, where the fiction was, that the possessor had obtained the ownership by *usucapion*, and so was *quasi ex jure Quiritium dominus;* and he also aided parties by *exceptiones* and *in integrum restitutio*."

143. "The old forms of procedure were few in number, and they were often inconvenient, and failed to do justice. Accordingly, the prætor extended the remedies by action, as already intimated,

in the case of the *Publiciana actio.* This change probably commenced after many of the *legis actiones* were abolished by the *Æbutia lex*, and the necessity of new forms of actions arose. These were introduced by the prætors, and it is hardly a matter of doubt, that, in establishing the formulæ, they followed the analogy of the *legis actiones.* It is the conclusion of an ingenious writer,[1] 'that the edict of the *prætor urbanus* was, in the main part relating to actions, arranged after the model of the old *legis actiones*, and that the system is apparent in the code of Justinian, and still more in the digest.'"

144. The edicts of the prætors, after they had thus become established as law, underwent some change prior to the date of Justinian's compilations. Under the emperors, commentaries were written on the edict, which were works of considerable extent; one of which, — a commentary by Labeo, on the edict of the strangers' prætor, — is mentioned as consisting of no less than thirty books.

145. When the practice of imperial rescripts, which will be described hereafter, became established, it seems, that the practice of making annual edicts became less common, and that, probably after the time of Adrian, it fell into disuse; though the edict still remained in force, as an important, indeed the most important, branch of the law.

---

[1] Rhein. Mus. für Juris. I. p. 51, *Die Œconomie des Edictes* von Heffter.

146. In the reign of Adrian, and probably by his direction, the edict was revised, and reduced to systematic form, by Salvius Julianus, a distinguished jurist, who had filled the office of prætor. This work of Julian,—in which all the old edicts were collected and arranged, obsolete parts left out or abridged, and the whole put in order,—was denominated the *edictum perpetuum.* It exercised a great influence on the study of the law, and on subsequent juridical writings, and was observed as authoritative in the courts of justice. It is this work which is so frequently mentioned in the digest as the edict.

147. Other magistrates, besides the city and strangers' prætors, exercised the right of making edicts in the manner already described, as, for example, the curule ediles, who had jurisdiction, among other things, of matters relating to the public streets. All these edicts are supposed to have been incorporated in the work of Julian.

148. The edict is sometimes called in the digest the *jus honorarium*, on account of the honors to which those magistrates were entitled, by whom it was established. "It is from this honorary law," says Pothier,[1] "that the Roman law has derived its principal lustre. The civil right, if separated from the honorary, would be too severe; and, if applied according to the rigor of the principles upon which

[1] Prolegomena in Pandectas Justinianeas, Part I. Cap. III. Art. IV.

it is founded, as expressed in the terms in which its provisions are conceived, it would frequently be contrary to equity. The honorary law, the growth of experience, and more accommodated to times, places, and persons, is less subtle, more just, and more proper for the government of men. The prætor, in tempering the severity of the civil right, always preserves the respect which is due to the law, and renders it more equitable by an interpretation, which, affecting only the terms of the law, moderates the law itself, without appearing to change its spirit."

149. The manner in which the law, properly so called, was supplied, assisted, and corrected, by the prætor's edict, will be best explained and illustrated by examples, of which the digest contains a great number. The three following are among those given by Pothier:[1] —

150. I. When a father died intestate, his estate devolved upon his proper heirs, that is, his children; but, according to the strict law, emancipated children were excluded from all participation in the succession, because the act of emancipation put them out of the family. But an emancipated child continues, notwithstanding, to be the child of his father, and neither emancipation nor any other technical ground of law can destroy the natural right of a child to share in the paternal inheritance.

---

[1] Prolegomena in Pandectas Justinianeas, Part I. Cap. III. Art. IV.

151. The prætor, therefore, in order to make this natural right effectual, introduced or admitted a fiction, by which it was supposed, that the act of emancipation was rescinded by the death of the father, and that the emancipated child was thereby restored to the family. Having thus got the child back into the family, the prætor allowed him to share with the other children in the estate of his parents.

152. But in doing this the prætor took care to respect the letter of the law. He did not allow the emancipated child to inherit by a right of property, which, it was conceived, the law alone could give, and which the fiction of the prætor did not pretend to reach or affect. He simply gave the heir a right of possession, which, however, was equally effectual as a right of property would have been; because, as the remedial law[1] was entirely in the hands of the prætor, he could defend the heir in the possession and enjoyment of his distributive share. This right of possession, therefore, is not the right of an heir, though it differs but little from it, and has the same effect. The prætorian right of succession, if such it may be called, was denominated the *bonorum possessio*, which the prætor gave to those who were

---

[1] That is, the granting or withholding of an action for a supposed injury, or the allowing or refusing of a particular matter, as a ground of defence to an action.

not entitled by the strict law to a share of the inheritance.

153. II. A acquires from B, by a just title, and, in good faith, a thing which is the property of C; and, before he has been in the enjoyment of the thing, for a sufficient length of time to become the owner by prescription, he is dispossessed of it by a stranger. In this case, A is not entitled to maintain an action against the stranger by whom he has been evicted, even if the eviction is unjust, because, according to the strict law, no one but the proprietor of the thing sought to be recovered can bring an action to recover it. Equity, however, requires that one who has acquired and is in possession of a thing in good faith should be preferred to an unjust possessor, or, as we should say, to a mere wrongdoer.

154. In order to accomplish this, the prætor first established the principle, that, as against a mere wrongdoer, the possession for any length of time in good faith is equivalent to a possession for the whole period of prescription, and, by this fiction, supplied the time which was wanting to ripen the possession of A into a right of property. Having done this, it would seem, that there could be no difficulty in allowing A to maintain the same action to which he would have been entitled, according to the strict law, as the proprietor.

155. But this would be a proceeding, by which

one of the received forms of action would be extended to a case not contemplated by the law; because, although the prætor had put the possessor in good faith upon the same footing with a proprietor, he could not make him a proprietor, in fact, without running the risk of depriving the real owner of his right of property, which would be contrary both to law and equity; and, therefore, the prætor introduced a new form of action denominated *utile*, for the use and benefit of the *bonâ fide* possessor, which was allowed to have the same effect, relative to such possessor, as the action *in rem* would have in favor of the true proprietor.

156. By this mode of proceeding, the equitable right of the possessor in good faith was rendered effectual, at the same time that the legal right of the real owner was preserved, against one who had no claim either in law or equity. In this manner, originated that large class of actions, of which frequent mention is made in the books of Roman law, under the head of *actiones utiles*.

157. III. A minor under twenty-five years of age, and past the age of puberty, is deceived into the purchase of a thing, for a price much exceeding its value. The law requires that he should perform his agreement, because it looks upon him as capable of entering into a contract. But equity demands, nevertheless, that the seller, in such a case, should not be allowed to take advantage, in order to enrich himself, of the buyer's inexperience.

158. The prætor, therefore, had recourse to an expedient, by which, while he respected the law of the contract, he was enabled to do justice between the parties. He admitted the legal obligation of the contract, because the law declared it to be valid; but at the same time he prevented the seller from enforcing it by action, or relieved the buyer, if the contract had already been performed, by restoring the parties to the same situation, in which they were previously to the making of the contract. Such is the origin of that class of proceedings, known by the name of *restitutio in integrum*, by means of which a contract or transaction is rescinded, so as to place the parties to it in the same position, with respect to one another, which they occupied before the contract was made or the transaction took place.

159. The edict, after its revision by Julian, became a fruitful subject for the commentaries of the jurists, and also a model for other juridical writings which did not bear that appellation; and, ultimately, these writings became of more authority, and more applicable in practice, than the edict itself; so that when the compilation of Justinian was made, the edict was not inserted therein, *eo nomine*, though the writings of the jurists upon it form a considerable portion of the digest. Some few fragments of the ancient edicts are extant; but, it is chiefly from the quotations and references contained in the writings of the jurists inserted in the digest, that we have any knowledge of the edict in its latest form.

Several attempts have been made to bring the fragments together into a connected form, and then to reconstruct the perpetual edict as revised by Julian.[1]

160. In order to enable the reader to form some idea of the style of this branch of the Roman jurisprudence, as well as of the relation which it bore, in point of form, to the strict law, it is proposed to give a translation of several passages of it, as they occur in the digest.

161. Having already given a specimen of the laws of the twelve tables, by a translation of those contained in the first table, concerning citation in justice, it will help us to judge of the relation of the prætorian to the strict law, to insert a translation of some of those parts of the edict which relate to the same matter. The following are provisions of this kind:—

162. "Let no person cite in justice (*in jus*,) his father, or his mother, his patron, or his patroness, or their children, or parents, without my express permission."

"If any one shall contravene this prohibition, I will condemn him to a penalty of fifty pieces of gold, if it is demanded within the year."

"Whoever is cited *in jus*, for any cause, ought to obey the summons."

"If any one is cited *in jus*, and does not present

---

[1] The most recent, of which I have seen any notice, is by C. G. L. de Weyhe, published in 1821.

himself accordingly, I will coerce him to do so by a fine, upon cognizance of the cause."

"When one is cited *in jus*, who is exempted therefrom by the edict, he is under no obligation, nor shall he be compelled, to appear."

"Let no one, by violence or by fraud, carry away a person who is summoned *in jus*."

"If any one shall disobey this injunction, I will give an action against him *in factum*."

"If any one shall cite *in jus*, his father, or his mother, his patron, or his patroness, or their father, mother, or children, or his own children, or any other person whom he shall have in his power, as his wife, or his son's wife, he shall receive such sureties (*fidejussores*) for them as they shall offer."

"I will decree a penalty of fifty pieces of gold against one who shall refuse such sureties."

"I will give against him who shall become surety (*fidejussor*), for the appearance of another *in jus*, an action to recover the value of the thing in dispute."

"I will not force the proprietors of immovables to give sureties; but I will compel them to take an oath to present themselves."

"If any one is unable to give surety at Rome, and requests that the cause may be removed to the city where he resides, I will remit it accordingly, upon cognizance of the affair, in order that the party may there give his surety; provided he shall first take an oath that he does not make the demand fraudulently, or for the purpose of annoying his adversary."[1]

163. Various other provisions, relating to the same subject, are found among the fragments of the edict. Those above given will show the mode, in which the prætor was accustomed to supply the deficiencies of the strict law.

164. It is quite apparent, from the foregoing description of the law introduced by the prætor's edict, that, in its essential elements of assisting, supplying, and correcting the positive law, it bore a strong resemblance to that portion of the remedial law of England and of this country, which is denominated equity. In the mode of proceeding, the two systems differed altogether. The forms of action established by the prætor, for the prosecution of injuries, for which the law had provided no remedy by action, were strictly analogous to the established forms; while the proceedings in equity, under the English system, are wholly different, in point of form, from the methods practised in the courts of law. In this respect, the authority conferred by the statute of Edward I. upon the clerks in chancery, for the framing of writs *in like cases* to those for which a form was already provided, is much more analogous to that exercised by the prætor.

165. In another respect, also, there was a differ-

---

[1] The foregoing provisions of the Perpetual Edict are taken from the Prolegomena to Pothier's Pandects.

ence between the two systems. The judgments, which resulted from the prætorian actions, were the same in point of form as those which followed an action framed upon the strict law. But, according to the English system, the decree in equity has other purposes, and is executed in a measure wholly different, from a judgment at law. These differences have served to keep the two systems of law and equity in England entirely distinct from each other, and to cause them to be administered by different courts; whereas, in Rome, the analogy or identity of the proceedings under the prætorian, and under the strict positive law, had the effect ultimately to blend the two together into one homogeneous system.

166. The prætorian law, and the system of equity in England, have this in common, that by supplying, assisting, and correcting the strict law without the aid of legislation, properly so called, they have made the administration of justice coextensive with the necessities of an active, industrious, and prosperous community.

167. The history of the Roman law, as it has thus far been traced, serves to show how, in the progress of time, the legal polity of a state takes the form alternately of legislation or positive law, and of jurisprudence. Before the enactment of the twelve tables, the Romans appear to have been governed by customs and unwritten laws, which, to a considerable extent, corresponded with what we

have denominated jurisprudence. These laws and usages were reduced into a fixed form, and, with other analogous provisions, became the positive law established in the twelve tables. The twelve tables then became the framework for a vast accretion of jurisprudence, in the form of the prætorian edict. The latter at length took the form of positive law, and itself became the nucleus of commentaries, judicial exposition, and other forms of jurisprudence, which, in their turn, assumed a fixed and positive state in the digest of Justinian. The latter, then, the student of Roman law will have occasion to observe, became a text for jurisprudence to an extent, which, if we had not before us the immense mass of English and American reports, would almost exceed our powers of belief. Out of the jurisprudence which was thus formed around the fragments of the great Roman jurists, preserved in the compilations of Justinian, have been extracted in modern times much of the material for the French and other codes of positive law, which are rapidly and constantly undergoing the same process of enlargement and extension.

SECTION V.—*Jurisconsults and Jus Respondendi.*

168. The origin among the Romans of a body of men, who were expounders of the law, is attributed to the publication of the forms of actions by Flavius,

which extended the knowledge and the practice of the law to the plebeians. The brevity and conciseness of the laws of the twelve tables rendered interpretation necessary. At first, the decemvirs, by whom they had been compiled, were the interpreters. Afterwards, this function devolved upon the college of pontiffs, one of whom was assigned every year to answer the questions of individuals relative to matters of law.

169. This state of things, in which the law of religion, the *jus pontificium*, and the civil law, *jus civile*, were both intrusted to the interpretation of the same body of men, lasted for about a century. It was broken up, and the *jus civile* and the *jus pontificium* separated, as already remarked, by the publication of the Flavian law, after which all persons, who thought themselves and were deemed by others capable of it, decided questions of law, upon which they were consulted. The pontiffs still remained in the exclusive possession of the interpretation of the law of religion, which, from the earliest period in the history of Rome, was a matter of great interest and importance, and the *auctoritas pontificium* continued to have the same operation and effect, with respect to the law of religion, that the *auctoritas prudentium* had in the civil law.

170. While these two functions were united in the pontiffs, they gave *responsa de omnibus divinis et humanis rebus;* after the separation they retained the former, and the latter fell into the hands of the

jurisconsults. This will enable us to understand the definition given by Ulpian, and inserted in Justinian's institutes, of the term jurisprudence, namely, that it "is the knowledge of things divine and human; the science of what is just and unjust."[1]

171. When the separation between the civil law and the law of religion had thus been effected, every one, who saw fit to do so, became an interpreter of the civil law; and, at length, those who were the most skilful, and the most frequently consulted, formed a body of men who devoted themselves to jurisprudence as a profession. Persons who thus made a business of interpreting the law were known by the various names of *jurisperiti*, *jurisconsulti*, or simply *consulti*. They were also designated as *jurisprudentes*, *prudentiores*, *peritiores*, and *juris auctores*. Cicero defines a *jurisconsult*, "a person who has such a knowledge of the laws (*leges*) and customs (*consuetudines*) which prevail in a state, as to be able to advise (*respondendum*), act (*agendum*), and to secure a person in his dealings (*cavendum*).

---

[1] This definition seems to have excited the special horror of Dr. Cooper, who, in a note on the passage in which it occurs, says, "This definition is very convenient for the alliance between church and state; an alliance that I hope will never take place in these States. I know of no things that ought to be kept more distinct, because they are so, than the affairs of this world and those of the world to come; nor do I know of any two things that despotism has so sedulously labored to intertwine." As above explained, the "alliance" between things "divine and human," in the definition of jurisprudence, seems to be not only harmless, but quite proper. See Cooper's Justinian, 404.

172. The business of the early jurisconsults was to advise their clients, and to act on their behalf, gratuitously. They gave their advice, or answers, either in public places, which they attended regularly at certain stated times, or at their own houses; and not only on matters of law, but on any topics that might be referred to their consideration. They were also employed in the drawing up of written instruments, as contracts and testaments. Many of these functions afterwards came to be performed by persons who received fees, and thus a body of practitioners arose distinct from those who gave *responsa*, and were writers and teachers. Besides their clients, the jurisconsults were attended by the students of law, who wrote down the answers which were given. Not only parties, but also judges, that is, those who were appointed by the magistrate to perform the duty of a judex, in the trial of an action, had recourse to the jurisconsults, and received their answers.[1]

173. This usage is said to have ceased or rather to have been modified under Augustus, who prohibited the jurisconsults from giving their answers, and from deciding questions of law, without being first authorized by the sovereign. The object of the emperor in this probably was to obtain a control over the administration of the law, which he could not obtain in any direct manner; and thus, by means

---

[1] These answers are frequently referred to in the digest.

of the jurisconsults, to bring about those changes in the old law which could not otherwise be effected. The example of Augustus was followed by his successors to the time of Adrian, who, as we are informed by Pomponius, reëstablished the jurisconsults in their full liberty of advice and consultation.

174. It seems, that, at first, the opinions of the jurisconsults had no other weight or authority than resulted from the number of those who agreed in sentiment, and from the general acquiescence of the people in the decisions which they promulgated. In time, however, these opinions being received and conformed to in practice, became, according to Pomponius, the source and origin of almost all the customs and usages which formed so considerable a branch of the civil law. At a later period the rule seems to have been, that the unanimous opinion of the jurists was to have the force of law; but, if they were not unanimous, the judex might follow which opinion he pleased. According to Gaius, this rule was established by Adrian. Perhaps it is more probable, that the rescript of that emperor, relating to this matter, was merely confirmatory of an established practice.

175. The constitution of this body, and their mode of proceeding, are not known. It is not unreasonable to suppose, that they formed a sort of college; or, at all events, that they met together at stated times for the purpose of forming and giving their opinions; otherwise, it could only be ascer-

tained what were their opinions as individuals. Their power of deciding was limited to the cases which actually came before them. The decision, however, would undoubtedly be regarded as a precedent, and serve as authority for future cases of the same kind.

176. The earlier jurisconsults gave their opinions either orally or in writing; and, in the time of Tiberius, *signata*, that is, in an official form. The question proposed was sometimes stated in the answer, either briefly or in full; and the answer sometimes contained the reasons upon which the opinion was founded; though it was equally valid without. The answers of the jurisconsults, thus given, became an acknowledged source of the law, denominated the *Responsa Prudentium.*

177. It seems, that in the earlier period of the history of the jurisconsults, they were accustomed to meet together near the temple of Apollo, for the discussion of questions upon which there was a difference of opinion among them. If, upon such discussion, and after weighing the reasons for and against the different opinions, they came to an unanimous result, their conclusion was denominated a received opinion; which, from thenceforth, was followed in all their future discussions, and also in the tribunals, and thus acquired the authority of a written law. The *Receptæ Sententiæ* are frequently referred to in the digest.

178. The discussions and opinions of the juris-

consults were probably the source of much of the prætorian law. But they appear also to have been the direct source of many additions to, or rather extensions of, the positive law, independently of the edict. The following are examples.[1]

179. I. According to the law of the twelve tables, when a *libertus* died intestate and without children, his patron, that is, his ancient master, was entitled to his succession, or, in other words, to the estate which he might leave. But the law was silent in regard to the guardianship of a *libertus*, who had not attained the age of puberty. The jurisconsults held, that, as equity required that he who is entitled to the advantage of a thing should also bear the burdens which belong to it, the law must be considered to have tacitly imposed the burden of guardianship upon him who was entitled to the inheritance, in case of the death of the minor.

180. II. The jurisconsults were the inventors of a great many of the forms of stipulation which were in use; one of which, called the *Aquilian* stipulation, derives its name from Aquilius Gallus, who was quite celebrated for his ingenuity in this respect. Acceptilation was a mode of extinguishing or discharging an obligation, by means of a solemn form of words; but which, according to a rule of Roman law, (as well as our own,) was not applica-

---

[1] These examples are taken from Pothier's Pandects, Proleg. cap. IV.

ble to obligations contracted in any other manner than by words. The device of Aquilius was a form of stipulation, by which every obligation, (even an obligation contracted *ex re*, as for example, a loan for use,) might first be converted into a verbal obligation, and then it became susceptible of being discharged by an acceptilation.

181. III. It was a rule of law, that grandchildren, born after the death of their father, in the lifetime of their grandfather, might nevertheless be instituted as the heirs of the latter. The jurisconsults extended this rule to the great-grandchildren, and also to all cases in which the son was out of the power of the testator, in whatever manner it might be. The introduction of this principle is attributed also to Aquilius.

182. IV. Many other jurists were the authors of means and supplements of the same kind. Such, for example, was the *cautio Muciana*, or form of engagement to be entered into by a surety, to be given by a legatee, before receiving a legacy which had been left to him on the condition of his not doing a particular thing. From the same source, also, are derived the form of testaments *per æs et librum*, that is, an imaginary sale, trusts, and other acts of the same nature. The jurisconsults appear also to have been the original inventors of those forms of action which were called *utiles*, or useful, to which allusion was made in connection with the prætor's edict.

183. The jurists, under the empire, are distinguished from those of the republic by two circumstances, namely, the *jus respondendi*, which has already been spoken of, and the formation of two sects or schools, which remain to be noticed.

SECTION VI. — *Rival Sects or Schools.*

184. It would have been strange indeed, if, with the freedom of discussion, which rendered the decisions of the jurisconsults so valuable, there had not been some important and radical differences of opinion among them; and accordingly we find, that even before the time of Cicero, the principal jurisconsults were not agreed upon the question, among others, whether the children of a slave were or were not the property of the master. But it was not until the time of Augustus, that these differences became so systematic as to constitute a division of the jurisconsults into two distinct schools or sects.

185. The founders of these two schools were respectively Ateius Capito and Antistius Labeo, neither of whom had the honor of giving his name to the sect which he established. The followers of Labeo were called Proculeians, from Proculus, one of his most distinguished disciples; those of Capito received the name of Sabinians from Sabinus; the former were also sometimes, though it seems, improperly, called Pegasians, and the latter Cassians.

It is stated by Mackeldy, that these schools appear to have been nothing more than separate academies or offices (*stationes*), for giving *responsa* or opinions. The names of the chiefs of each school, eight in number, from the time of Augustus to that of Adrian, — after which the distinction does not appear to have been kept up, — are given by Pomponius. The last of the Sabinians was Salvius Julianus, by whom the prætorian law was revised, and put into the form of the perpetual edict.

186. In studying the Roman law, it is quite important to have some general knowledge of the differences which existed between these two schools; inasmuch as their respective opinions are very frequently referred to and discussed by the jurists, whose writings are preserved in the digest; and an acquaintance with them will serve to explain, if not to reconcile, the seeming contradictions which the texts of the law occasionally present.

187. In order to convey some notion of these differences between the jurisconsults, and at the same time to explain the mode, as well as to show the temper and spirit, in which the Roman jurisconsults conducted their discussions, it will be useful to devote a few paragraphs to the subject of the rival schools. The most satisfactory and intelligible explanation of the principles, upon which the division was founded, is given by a late French author, already referred to, from whose work the following

account of the characteristic differences between the two sects is translated.[1]

188. "The original cause of division among the jurisconsults was the introduction of the philosophy of Greece, (especially the doctrines of the stoics,) into the science of the law. One party warmly embraced the new philosophy, and borrowed from it every thing which could be applied to jurisprudence. The other resisted the movement, and held on to the doctrines and maxims which they had received from their predecessors. Such is the fundamental difference, which Pomponius states to have existed between Capito and Labeo, and which may doubtless be ascribed to their respective schools: *Ateius Capito in his, quæ ei tradita fuerant, perseverabat, Labeo ingenii qualitate, et fiducia doctrinæ, qui et in ceteris operis sapientiæ operam dederat, plurima innovare instituit:* Capito adhered to the received doctrines; Labeo, confident in himself, and imbued with the new philosophy, was in favor of innovations."

189. "Philosophy is sometimes looked upon as only another name for equity, or the law of reason. Hence, it was concluded that Labeo modified the ancient jurisprudence by equity; and the dispute

---

1 Élémens de Droit Romain, par Heineccius; Traduits, Annotes, Corrigés et Précedés d'une Introduction Historique, par M. Ch. Giraud, a Paris, 1835. The translation is taken from page 311, and following.

between the two sects was regarded as a struggle between equity and strict right. But, admitting this to be true, it would be found not a little embarrassing to decide, which of the two sects held to the rigorous interpretation of the law, and which admitted that of justice and benevolence; for, if it should be presumed, on the one hand, from the justly-acquired reputation of Labeo as a philosopher, that he would be more ready to depart from the strict sense of the law; and if, on the other, the deference of Capito for the ancients should cause him to be regarded as the slave of texts and traditions; these conjectures would not be at all confirmed by an examination of the facts; inasmuch as it is frequently impossible to decide, from the particular cases of these differences which have been transmitted to us, on which side the equity is."

190. "Indeed, we are sometimes compelled to inquire, whether equity had any thing whatever to do with the question; and, in fact, if we examine the cases carefully, with a view to determine on which side equity exists, we shall be compelled to decide more frequently for the disciples of Capito, than for those of Labeo. It has thus happened, that the character of defenders of equity has been accorded by one set of celebrated authors to the Proculeians, and by another to the Sabinians. This, however, was not the ground of the dissension between the sects; it was not the exclusive system of either

to substitute the rules of equity for those of positive law."

191. "The philosophy of the stoics was eminently moral; but it was especially remarkable for its inflexible logic. We learn, from the writers who have transmitted to us the opinions and the actions of the most illustrious philosophers of this sect, that they were distinguished particularly for the closeness of their reasonings, for their constant habit of investigating the principles of things, and for their inflexible sagacity in carrying out an admitted or established principle to its ultimate consequences. Such were the stoics in philosophy; and such was Labeo in jurisprudence. What he borrowed from them was not so much their principles, as their mode of reasoning; not so much their system of morals, as of logic. He also imitated the stoics in his attachment to philology, in his study of etymologies, and in his attempt to give language the strictness of mathematics."

192. "The effect of such an alliance of philosophy with jurisprudence was not to modify the law by equity, but, on the contrary, to render it an exact science, to coördinate all its different parts, and to bring its special rules into strict conformity with its general principles. Labeo, instead of following the opinions of the ancients, confidently adopted the conclusions, which his subtle and penetrating mind deduced from established principles. His character is

indicated by Pomponius in the words, *ingenii qualitate, et fiducia doctrinæ.* The confidence of Labeo in his doctrine, partakes of the mathematician; and if there is any foundation for the remark of Leibnitz, that the Roman jurisconsults resembled the mathematicians, it is because there was but little difference between the logic of mathematics, and the logic of the stoics."

193. "Capito, who was more strictly devoted to the customary and practical jurisprudence, did not undertake to explain the letter of the law, but to reproduce the opinions of the ancients: *In his, quæ ei tradita fuerant, perseverabat,* he taught that which he had himself been taught."

194. "The difference, therefore, between the methods of these two masters, was, that the one started from logic, and the other from authority; but it did not follow that the object of the first was equity, and that of the other strict law; inasmuch as logic and the authority of tradition are both ways which may lead, indifferently, sometimes to the one and sometimes to the other. Labeo admitted neither equity nor strict law, but only when the one or the other was the natural consequence of the principles from which he started. Capito admitted the one or the other in every question, according as the ancients, in treating of the subject, had proceeded upon grounds of equity or of strict law. It may be presumed, however, that equity would most frequently be found on the side of the theories of Labeo."

195. "The characteristics which distinguished the respective chiefs of the two schools, according to Pomponius, were, in short, that Labeo, who possessed an enlarged and liberal mind, and was a subtle dialectitian and a bold innovator, subjected every thing to the test of his logic, whilst Capito, a learned but timid and modest man, followed respectfully in the tracks of his predecessors."

196. "Politics, also, had something to do with these divisions of the jurists. Labeo was an ardent republican; but of that good company who had been the means of introducing the Greek philosophy into Rome, and of sustaining it there. Augustus respected him, and did honor both to his talents and his character. Capito, on the contrary, was far from leaving behind him the noble character, and the well-established reputation, of his rival. He was the flatterer of power, and made himself its slave. The system of Labeo partook of the large and generous spirit for which he was distinguished, and which, in general, is characteristic of every political opposition; that of his rival, on the contrary, reflected the coldness, the tendency towards materialism, and the inclination for the dogma of passive obedience, which belonged to his character. It is not improbable, that political differences had a great influence in establishing the profound distinction which separated the two schools."

197. Having thus explained the origin of the rival schools, and pointed out the principles upon which

they first differed, it will be interesting now to see, what were the kind of questions which afterwards arose between them, and what were the grounds upon which the partisans of each placed their respective opinions. The following are examples of these differences.

198. I. In order to determine the age of puberty, the Sabinians, who adhered to ancient customs, were in favor of an examination in each particular case; the Proculeians, regarding such a proceeding as indecent, fixed upon fourteen as the age of puberty in persons of the male sex; and this became the established rule.[1]

199. II. According to the Proculeians, a condition, which was contrary to good manners, or was impossible to be performed, rendered the act or contract to which it was annexed null and void in every case. The Sabinians, on the contrary, made a distinction. They admitted this result in all acts between living persons; but, in testaments, they considered such a condition as not written, that is, they held it to be void.

200. III. It was made a question, whether the giving of one thing for another was a sale. The Sabinians decided that it was, because it was of no consequence, whether the price of a thing sold consisted of a sum of money or of some other thing of

---

[1] Giraud, Introduction Historique, 319. The remaining examples are taken from Pothier's Pandects, Proleg. Part. II. Cap. II. § 2.

equal value. The jurisconsults of the other sect were of a different opinion, and held that a money price was necessary to constitute a contract of sale, and this opinion prevailed. The question seems a very trifling one to us, but it had some importance among the Romans, as connected with the actions which resulted from the contract of sale.

201. IV. If a stake-holder refused to deliver the stake to the winner, the Sabinians held, that the winner might prosecute him as a thief, not only for the part deposited as a winner, but also for that deposited by the loser, on the ground that the latter belonged equally to the winner. The Proculeians, whose opinion prevailed, maintained the contrary, on the ground that theft was a fraudulent usurpation of another's possession, and that the winner never had either the ownership or the possession of that part of the deposit which was contributed by the loser.

202. V. If one person should inflict a mortal wound upon a slave, and, afterwards, another person should kill him, the Proculeians were of opinion, that the first was liable for the wounding only, and the second for the killing; because, according to the strict signification of the word *kill*, it was the second and not the first that was guilty, although the latter had in fact inflicted a wound that would have been mortal, if it had not been for the act of the other. The Sabinians maintained that both parties were guilty, because they had both really killed the slave

at different times. The first opinion was adopted by Ulpian, and received the sanction of the digest.

203. VI. The two schools were at issue upon the question, whether the earnings or other acquisitions of a slave, who had absconded, belonged to the master. The Sabinians, recognizing the principle, that a runaway slave continued, notwithstanding, to be the property of his master, held the affirmative. The Proculeians took the other side, on the ground, that, inasmuch as the master had no power in fact over the slave himself, he could not hold or acquire any thing by the act of the slave. This opinion was rejected.

204. VII. If one of several partners should receive a wound, in endeavoring to stop the flight of certain slaves belonging to the partnership, it was the opinion of Labeo, that the wounded partner could not recover the expense of his cure from the partnership, because the expense was not incurred *by* the partnership, though it was incurred *for* the the partnership. It is hardly necessary to say, that this opinion was rejected.

205. VIII. The question, as to the ownership of an article made by one person of materials belonging to another, is usually given as an illustration of the influence of the stoic philosophy upon the discussions of the schools. Nerva and Proculus were of opinion that the thing made belonged to the maker; as, for example, if any one should make wine from the grapes of another, or should cast a

vessel out of metal that belonged to another, the wine or the vessel would belong to the maker; for the reason, that the thing made had never previously belonged to any body. In this they followed the principle of the stoics, that a thing perishes by a change of form; from whence it followed, that as the form of the grapes and of the metal had disappeared, the wine and the vessel were new things, which belonged to the maker, since every thing which exists is what it is by reason of its form. The Sabinians were of opinion, that it was much more just and natural to reason, that the owner of the matter continued to be the owner of the thing made, because, without the matter, which belonged to him, the new form given to it could not have existed.

206. Justinian decided this question, in his institutes,[1] by adopting what he calls the middle opinion, of those who thought that if the thing could be reduced to its original materials, it belonged to the owner of the materials, but, that if it could not be so reduced, it belonged to the maker. According to this principle, the wine, in the case supposed, would belong to the maker, the casting to the owner of the metal.

207. These examples have been selected from many others, because they are likely to be intelligible, without any particular knowledge of the tech-

---

[1] Lib. II. t. 1, § 25.

nicalities of Roman law. They will suffice to give some idea of the nature of the questions which divided the lawyers, as well as of the sort of discussions which occur in their writings. It should be remarked, in conclusion, that these differences of opinion are, for the most part, preserved in the digest as historical facts merely, and that they have had but little effect to render the law itself uncertain or obscure.

208. In the reign of Adrian, and especially after the revision of the perpetual edict, which probably settled a great many controverted points, the disputes of the schools began to subside, and very soon disappeared altogether. It was supposed, by some of the older writers on the Roman law, that, about this time a new sect arose, which partook of the opinions of both the others, and in fact superseded them; but this is now considered to be an erroneous conjecture; inasmuch as the old schools lingered for some time after the reign of Adrian, and there had previously been jurists who adopted the opinion of both indifferently.

209. Besides the *responsa*, which have been spoken of, the jurisconsults were the authors of commentaries on the laws of the twelve tables, the edict, and on particular laws, and on the works of one another. They also wrote treatises of an elementary character, such as the institutes of Gaius, which was the earliest work of the kind; books known as rules and definitions; collections of

cases and answers; and many other works, with various titles, such as disputations, questions, manuals, &c.

SECTION VII. — *Law of Citation.*

210. The only other circumstance connected with the jurisconsults, which requires to be mentioned, is what is called the *law of citation*. We have already seen the authority, which, for a considerable period, was attributed to the answers of the living jurists. In the year 426, when this source of jurisprudence had become superseded by imperial rescripts, a similar character was conferred on the writings of certain of the great jurists of preceding generations.[1] The law of citation was an imperial constitution, bearing the names of Theodosius the younger and Valentinian III. but generally attributed to the latter only. By this constitution the works of five authors, namely, Papinian, Paul, Gaius, Ulpian, and Modestinus, and of the jurists upon whose works they had commented, were selected from the great mass of juridical writings, and were invested with the authority of law.

211. If, upon the examination of any question,

---

[1] The emperor Constantine, a century previous, seems to have found it necessary to determine, by special ordinances, what writings of the old jurists should have authority, and what should not be regarded as authoritative. Giraud, Introduction Historique, 358.

there was found to be any difference of opinion among the five, that of the majority was to govern. If they were equally divided, that is, if one of them had not expressed any opinion, upon a given question, the opinion, which had Papinian in its favor, was to be taken; if he had expressed no opinion, then it was the duty of the judex to adopt whichever opinion he might think proper. If the correctness of the text of an author was called in question, it was to be rectified by a collation of the best manuscripts.

212. This law seems to have made a part of the legal reform, contemplated by Theodosius, and which was partially effected by means of the code, which bears his name. The law of citation is said not to have entirely fulfilled the purposes which it had in view, and Justinian, in his commission to Tribonian and his associates, for the compilation of the digest, directs them not to be governed by the majority, where there was a difference of opinion among the writers, but to exercise their own judgment.

SECTION VIII. — *Imperial Rescripts and Decrees.*

213. The imperial rescripts constitute the only remaining topic which requires to be considered under the head of jurisprudence. When the entire authority of government had been assumed by the

emperors, they not only exercised the functions of legislators but also administered justice in the last resort. Every instrument, by which the imperial will was expressed, whatever might be the subject of it, was properly denominated a constitution.

214. If, however, the subject was not of general interest, the constitutions bore different appellations. Mandates (*mandata*) were the instructions of the emperor to public functionaries of various kinds. Decrees (*decreta*) were the decisions pronounced by the emperor, upon appeal from the sentences of inferior courts to the council, consistory, or auditory, of the prince. Rescripts (*rescripta*) were the opinions upon cases of doubt, or the answers to questions proposed, given by the emperor upon the application of a party, in which he either applied the existing law, or some analogy, or decided merely according to his will and pleasure.

215. The legal authority of rescripts and decrees was confined to the cases for which they were made. But if they were founded in sound principles of law, they were of course regarded as judicial precedents. The rescripts appear to have become a substitute, in a great degree, for all other forms of jurisprudence, and to have increased in numbers as the empire went to decay.

CHAPTER V.

REVISION OF THE ROMAN LAW BY THE EMPEROR JUSTINIAN.

216. THE foregoing sketch of the history of the Roman law, anterior to the time of Justinian, though necessarily general and imperfect, will give some idea of the great mass of materials out of which his compilations were made, and of the somewhat heterogeneous system, for which they were intended as a substitute. The merit of accomplishing a great and useful work must be ascribed to Justinian. But he cannot be regarded as the originator of the plan, upon which his reforms were effected. For his code, he had before him as models, the Gregorian, Hermogenian, and Theodosian; for the digest, the great jurists had already furnished him with examples, in the various works of the same kind executed on a more limited plan, and especially the work of Julian on the edict; and for his institutes, he not only borrowed the plan, but actually appropriated, as he himself states, the work itself, of Gaius.

SECTION I. — *First Edition of the Code.*

217. Justinian commenced with the imperial constitutions. In the year 528, of the christian era, he appointed a commission of ten lawyers, with directions to make a selection, from all the constitutions of his predecessors, including those contained in the three preceding codes, of such as were conformed to the usages of the times; to introduce such alterations and additions as were necessary; and to arrange the whole under appropriate titles. The work was very soon (in fourteen months) completed, in twelve books, and being confirmed and promulgated, took the place of all the previous legislation of the same kind. This first code, now known as the *codex vetus*, is no longer in existence.

SECTION II. — *Digest or Pandects.*

218. When the code had been completed, Justinian (A. D. 530) appointed a second commission, consisting of seventeen eminent jurists, at the head of whom was Tribonian, who had been a member of the former commission, to perform a similar task for the writings of the old jurists, which had just been executed for the constitutions of the emperors.

219. The commissioners were directed, in the first place, to read and correct (*elimare*, to file, polish,)

all the works of the ancient jurisconsults which were considered as authoritative, and to compose therefrom a body of jurisprudence, which should contain nothing superfluous or contradictory, and which should take the place of all the other books of law. They were to exclude altogether from the collection, those works which had neither been authorized by the imperial authority, nor sanctioned by usage.

220. The commissioners were further instructed to divide their work into fifty books, and each book into a number of titles, according to the order which had been already adopted in the code, or that of the perpetual edict, as they should think most proper; and to make their selections without regard to the law of citation already referred to; all the jurisconsults, whose decisions they should adopt, being regarded as of equal authority. They were to retrench every thing superfluous, to correct what was imperfect or defective, and to be careful to admit no contradiction. The new collection was to bear the name of digest or pandects. The emperor also announced his intention to direct the compilation of another work, in the form of institutes, for the use of students.

221. Justinian was not content with thus compiling a body of law. He wished, also, to prevent the necessity of such a work from ever recurring; and, therefore, prohibited the jurisconsults from daring to encumber his work with those verbose interpreta-

tions with which their predecessors had inundated the civil law.[1]

222. In the execution of their task, for which they were allowed ten years, but which was completed in three, the commissioners, as we are informed, extracted from the different writings of thirty-nine authors all that they considered valuable for the purposes of their compilation. A learned German professor,[2] with the patient diligence of his class, has investigated, and at length discovered, the plan upon which the commissioners proceeded with their work.

223. The editors of the pandects divided into three classes all the books from which extracts were to be made, and formed themselves into three sections; the first section read and extracted from the works on the *jus civile*, to which belonged the *libri ad Sabinum;* the second section extracted from the books on the prætorian edict, especially from Ulpian *ad edictum;* and the third section, from practical and casuistical writings, especially from the *Responsa* of Papinian, and the *Quæstiones* of Paulus. Three branches of extracts were thus formed, the Sabinus branch, the edict branch, and the Papinian

---

[1] Notwithstanding this prohibition, and, almost as it were, in mockery of it, the number of commentaries, which have been written on this one work, probably very much exceeds the number of those which were in existence in the time of Justinian.

[2] Dr. F. Bluhme, in the Zeitschrift für geschichtliche Rechtswissenschaft, 4ter Band, 257.

branch. From these three branches, the single titles of the pandects were composed.

224. The foundation of each title was generally formed by that branch, which furnished the most numerous and important fragments. After this, both the smaller branches were collated with it, the repetitions occurring in them were stricken out, the contradictions reconciled, and the necessary additions made; that which remained of the two latter branches was placed after the first, in such a manner, that the greater number of extracts was to decide, which of these should be placed in the middle and which at the end of the title. Hence arose the difference in the order of the three branches in the different titles. Every title does not, however, contain fragments from all the three branches, but only the larger titles; and in some of these the three branches even appear twice over. Though the course above described was the regular order of arrangement of the single fragments, there are nevertheless many exceptions.[1]

225. The quantity of the materials, which were made use of in the compilation of the digest, if the subject is closely examined, will not appear to be so vast as at first view. The amount doubtless seemed greater in the time of Justinian than a much larger quantity would to us at the present day. We have, however, some facts given us, by which we can de-

[1] Mackeldy: Lehrbuch des heutigen Roemischen Rechts, § 63.

termine very nearly the quantity of matter submitted by Justinian to his commissioners, compared with works of modern times. It is stated, that nearly two thousand treatises,[1] containing three millions of lines, were reduced to one hundred and fifty thousand lines in the digest. Assuming that the digest contains the one hundred and fifty thousand lines, then the whole collection was twenty times the size of the digest. In Beck's edition of the Corpus Juris Civilis, which is in octavo, the digest consists of two thousand and eighty-three pages, which number multiplied by twenty is equal to forty-one thousand six hundred and sixty pages, or fifty-two octavo volumes of eight hundred pages each. The whole collection, therefore, might be about twice the size of the octavo edition of Viner's Abridgment.

226. This mass was not to be digested, that is, condensed and abridged, as a volume of reports is treated at the present day; but the commissioners were to read the works before them and make extracts therefrom of those passages which they thought proper to retain. Keeping this direction in view, and recollecting, also, that the commissioners worked upon a plan which admitted of a division of labor, it does not seem very extraordinary, that the com-

---

[1] This perhaps refers not to treatises, but to the number of books, (that is, divisions of treatises,) inasmuch as the number of the latter, exclusive of those which consisted of more than one book, and the number of the books in which is not stated, amounts to one thousand seven hundred and forty-one.

missioners (seventeen in number) should have completed their task in three years. The alterations and additions, which they made in conformity with the emperor's directions, were probably not so extensive as to have occupied much time. The pandects were published on the 16th of December, A. D. 533, but were not to have the authority of law until the 30th of the same month.[1]

SECTION III. — *Institutes.*

227. Before the publication of the pandects, Justinian directed Tribonian, and two other jurists, to prepare an elementary treatise, under the name of institutes, for the use of students. This was completed and published on the 21st of November, A. D. 533, and received the force of law at the same time with the pandects.

228. The institutes, as already remarked, were a mere revision of the commentaries of Gaius, which had previously been used as an elementary work for beginners, but which, to some extent, had become inapplicable and obsolete. In making the revision, the work was brought into conformity with the existing state of things. The original commenta-

[1] The number of authors referred to is 107; those from whom extracts are taken, 39; number of treatises of the latter, 296; fragments, in all, 9143; from Ulpian, 2461; Paul, 2087; Papinian, 596; Pomponius, 588; Gaius, 536; Julian, 457, &c. See American Jurist, II. 63.

ries of Gaius having been discovered within a few years (1816), and restored to a very considerable extent, we have the means now at hand of comparing them with the institutes of Justinian, and of judging of the alterations and additions made by Tribonian. The process, employed by the latter, seems to be very much like that to which Mr. Sergeant Stephen has recently subjected Blackstone's commentaries.[1]

Section IV. — *New Code.*

229. When the institutes and pandects had been compiled and published, it appeared that the code was not entirely consistent with them, and, consequently, that further constitutions were necessary to bring the whole into harmony. Besides this, certain new constitutions, to the number of fifty, had been issued, for the decision of controverted questions, which were not comprised in the code. Justinian, therefore, directed Tribonian, and four other jurists, to make a revision of the code, and to add to it the new constitutions. The new work was very shortly completed, and, being confirmed November 16th, A. D. 534, the old code was abrogated. This col-

---

[1] After the publication of the institutes and digest, the sources from which they were compiled, being no longer of any practical utility, were neglected and lost, and very few fragments have come down to our times.

lection, denominated the *codex repetitæ prælectionis*, is the code now extant.

Section V. — *Novels.*

230. After the publication of the new code, in 535, Justinian continued to reign for thirty years, during which time he promulgated a great number of new constitutions, by which many changes in the law were effected. These were called *Novellæ*, or new constitutions. After the death of Justinian, a collection of 168 novels was made and published, 154 of which had been issued by him, and the others by his successors. The glossators, in the middle ages, divided the novels into nine collations, and each collation into several titles; but this division is no longer in use, and the novels are ordinarily distinguished by the order of their number.

231. Abstracts of those laws of the novels, which were enacted to complete or reform particular provisions of the code, for the preparation of which we are indebted to the interpreters of the middle ages, and principally to Irnerius, are inserted in the code, at the end of the laws to which they respectively relate. They are called the Authentics of the Code.

CHAPTER VI.

LAW SCHOOLS IN THE TIME OF JUSTINIAN.—LEGISLATION OF THE CONQUERORS OF THE WESTERN EMPIRE.—BASILICA.

232. HAVING thus given some account of the compilations of Justinian, such as they exist at the present day, it was next proposed to trace the progress of the Roman law since the time of Justinian; but, before proceeding to this part of the subject, there are three topics of which it will be proper here to take some notice.

SECTION I.—*Law Schools of Berytus and Constantinople.*

233. The first is the method of teaching the law before and at the time of Justinian.[1] In the time of Theodosius, there was but a single school of law in the western empire, which was at Rome, and did not survive the invasion of Italy by the barbarians.

---

[1] Giraud, Introduction Historique, 432.

This institution was merely a branch or faculty of the great academic establishment at the capital, which reckoned thirty-one professors, of whom only two were professors of law. In the east, the schools of Berytus and Constantinople enjoyed a great reputation. The mode of teaching which was practised in these schools, before the reform introduced by Justinian, was as follows.

234. The course of law required a period of five years for its accomplishment, three only of which were years of teaching, properly so called. The first year the pupils bore the name of *dupondii* (from *dupondium*, a small coin), as much as to say, persons of little account. During this year the institutes of Gaius, and certain other works of the same author, on particular topics, were explained to them, and the doctrines compared with those of other jurisconsults. The latter was a step towards a more profound and complicated study.

235. The pupils of the second year were called *edictales*, because they devoted themselves to the study of Ulpian's commentaries on the edict. Those of the third year were denominated *Papinianists*, because, in addition to the last parts of the edict, they studied the *Responsa* of Papinian. This title appears to have been an object of ambition to the students. The pupils of the fourth year were called *lytæ*, from the Greek λυται, *a nodis legumque ænigmatibus solvendis*. They then engaged among themselves in disputations upon the *Responsa* of

Paulus, under the direction of a professor. The pupils of the fifth year were named for the same reason *prolytæ*, from the Greek πϱολύται, because they continued the same exercise applied to the imperial constitutions.

236. This method was somewhat modified by the innovations and reforms of Justinian, but remained substantially the same. The pupils of the first year received the name of *Justinianists;* the institutes of Justinian, and the first four books of the digest were explained to them. Those of the second year preserved their name of *edictales;* but, instead of a commentary on the edict, they applied themselves to certain specified books of the digest, relating, in general, to contracts and the division of things.

237. The pupils of the third year preserved also the title of *Papinianists*, without, however, being engaged with the texts of Papinian; they then went back to the matters which had employed them during the first year, to which were added the 20th, 21st, and 22d books of the digest, which, on this account, were called *antepapinian.* The pupils of the fourth and fifth years also preserved their ancient denomination; but, as all the books of law, anterior to the time of Justinian, had become useless, by means of his legislation, the exercises of the students upon the *Responsa* of Paul, and upon the imperial rescripts, were replaced by particular passages extracted from certain different books of the digest, and from the code of Justinian.

SECTION II.—*Legislation of the Conquerors of the Western Empire.*

238. The second of the topics alluded to is the legislation of the barbarian conquerors of the western empire, before the accession of Justinian to the eastern. The Roman empire was divided into two, the eastern and western, in the year 364; the two were united under Theodosius the great, in 392, but were again separated on his death in 395, and so continued until the year 477, when the western was overthrown and destroyed by the barbarians. Justinian commenced his reign in the eastern in 527, fifty years afterwards; his legal reforms were completed in 535; and, in 554, he reconquered Italy, and there introduced his legislation.

239. During the intermediate period, between 477 and 554, the conquerors of the western empire, the Visigoths and Ostrogoths, had found it necessary to legislate for their Roman subjects, or rather for the new condition of things resulting from the mixture of the different races. This led to the compilation of the edict of Theodoric; the Roman law of the Visigoths, commonly designated by the name of the *Breviarium Alaricianum* or *Aniani*; the Roman law of the Burgundians, usually called the *Responsa Papiniani*, on account of its having been supposed, when first published, to be a fragment of Papinian. Several other works are also referred to this period,

as the *Mosaicarum et Romanarum Legum Collatio*, and the *Consultatio veteris jurisconsulti*.

240. These works are all interesting to the historian, and of some value to the student of Roman law. In the latter respect, they are curious as being compiled from some of the original sources, which were in existence before the work of Justinian, and which, not having been preserved by him in his collection, are almost wholly lost. This is particularly true of the Collation, the purpose of which was, by arranging fragments of the Roman law by the side of passages taken from scripture, and collating them together, to prove that the Roman law had its origin in the Mosaic. The work itself is, of course, of very little value.

SECTION III. — *Basilica*.

241. The above-mentioned works have been alluded to chiefly for the purpose of remarking, that though of some little value to the students of Roman law, they are of none at all in practice. For the same reason, it seems necessary to say a few words with reference to the state of the law in the eastern empire, after the revision by Justinian. The emperor's collections, being written in Latin, which was not in general use in the eastern empire, were immediately translated into Greek; and, the translations, though

not of an official character, soon came to be used more than the originals.

242. Justinian had prohibited all commentaries upon his laws ; but the prohibition was entirely disregarded, and commentaries were written and published upon them, in the Greek language, in great numbers. The consequence was, that, in little more than three centuries (A. D. 887), a new revision of the laws became necessary. This was undertaken by the emperor Basilius Macedo, and completed by his son Leo, the philosopher, and published in sixty books, under the title of the *Basilica.* The last named emperor issued many new constitutions, of which a collection was made by his order, consisting of 113 novels; which have been translated into Latin, and added as supplements to the Corpus Juris Civilis. Several other works of Romano-Greek law are in existence, which it seems unnecessary to mention.

243. The legislation of Justinian, as modified in the Basilica, continued to be the law in the eastern empire, until its destruction by the Turks, in the year 1453; and, even then, the Greeks, though subdued, were allowed to retain their own laws, as the Roman subjects of the barbarian conquerors of the western empire had been allowed to retain theirs. The Basilica, therefore, have remained to a very recent period, and, it is believed, are now, the foundation of the private laws of the Greeks. In 1830, a committee was appointed to revise the ancient

law, and to make a new code for Greece.[1] The Basilica, which has not come down to us in a perfect state, and the other writings of Roman Greek law, are of no other, or of little more, than a merely literary or historical value.

---

[1] What has been done, if any thing, in the accomplishment of this undertaking, I am not advised.

CHAPTER VII.

HISTORY OF THE ROMAN LAW, SINCE THE TIME OF JUSTINIAN.

244. The history of the Roman law, since the time of Justinian, if fully written, would be scarcely less than the history of human civilization for the same period; not that the latter is to be ascribed to the former, as its cause, but that, as the several nations of Europe, on emerging from the barbarism of the dark ages, went forward in civilization, the Roman law steadily accompanied them in their progress. In the western empire, which was in fact overthrown in 477, the collections of Justinian were promulgated as law, on the reconquering of Italy by him in the year 554, and were established and retained their authority as laws, in those parts only to which the authority of the emperors of the east extended, and for such brief time as that authority lasted.

245. But, under all the changes which took place in the countries which had constituted the empire of the west, the Roman law, as contained in these and

other collections which have already been mentioned, never went out of use. It was, at one time, generally supposed, and the fact is so stated by Blackstone,[1] that the Roman law, very soon after the revision by Justinian, "fell into neglect and oblivion, till about the year 1130, when a copy of the digest was found at Amalphi." But this statement is conclusively proved by Savigny, in his history of the Roman law in the middle ages,[2] to be entirely unfounded. It is true, that soon after the year 1130, the study of the Roman law revived, but not true, that the authority of it was ever lost; quite true, that the copy of the digest referred to was found at that time, but not true, that the different parts of Justinian's collection had previously disappeared altogether.

246. The preservation of the Roman law, as a law of custom and usage, where it had once been authoritative as legislation, seems to be partly due to a singular institution of the conquerors of the western empire. This was the system of *personal laws*, which deserves a single remark. The conquerors did not undertake either to exterminate the conquered people, or to amalgamate them with themselves, by imposing upon them the laws, manners,

---

[1] Comm. I. 81.

[2] Geschichte des Roëmischen Rechts im Mittelalter Von Friedrich Carl Von Savigny, Zweite Ausgabe, Heidelberg, 1834. This celebrated work is one of the chief monuments of the Historical School. See *post*, 266.

or language of Germany. The lands were divided between the conquerors and the conquered, but each nation preserved its laws and its organization. The Romans were allowed to retain their judiciary organization, their municipal administration, and the enjoyment of their civil law. The different nations thus lived together upon the same territory, without being confounded together, and each of them preserved its anterior institutions; and, when, in process of time, a fusion of the two races had taken place, it was found that the predominant character of the new society was much more Roman than German.

247. In France, in Italy, and Spain, the language and the legislation of the conquered had evidently prevailed over the religion, the language, and the laws of the conquerors. It was in reference to this system of personal laws that Agobard wrote to Louis le Debonnaire: "One frequently sees conversing together five persons, no two of whom are governed by the same laws."[1] It was in this way that the Roman law came to have force in many of the countries of Europe, by forming, originally and from the very first, the foundation, to a greater or less extent, of their social and civil institutions. In other portions of Europe, it attained the force of law in a somewhat different way, which will be mentioned presently.

---

[1] It is to this singular institution that we are probably indebted for

248. With the lapse of six centuries, from the downfall of the western empire, the ancient form of European civilization had disappeared, and, with the eleventh century, that of modern times had commenced its career. The new and advancing relations of society required further knowledge of the laws; and, as the necessity increased, the science was more and more studied, and a knowledge of the laws more and more diffused. In the twelfth century, to meet this growing want, a law school was established for the teaching of the Roman law, at Bologna; which was followed by others in other places, from whence the science became extended throughout Europe.

249. Two causes then began to operate, by means of which the Roman law attained greater authority in those countries where it had already been established, and was introduced into countries where it had previously had no legal authority. In the first place, it was a branch of polite learning, and as such made a part of the accomplishments of every educated person; and, secondly, the advancing civilization of the age was continually rendering the introduction of new law necessary, in almost every nation of Europe. It was entirely natural, therefore, that the system of Roman law, being perfectly adequate to the supply of every such want, and being

---

the origin of the term *Conflict of laws;* which has been superseded, in modern times by the more appropriate term, *International law.*

the only system in existence or known to anybody, should have been everywhere introduced for the purpose. The Roman law was also favored by the clergy, who gave their sanction on all occasions to its authority.

250. In one, or the other, or both, of the modes thus described, the Roman law has been much more widely extended in modern than the Roman empire ever was in ancient times. Its diffusion, from the middle ages to the present day, has taken place upon the simple principle, equally operative at this moment, that wherever, and whenever, and as to whatever, there was any want of its principles, for the regulation of human affairs, its authority has been at once recognized, admitted, and applied. An example of the introduction and application of the principles of the Roman law occurs with reference to the institution of domestic slavery in this country. Wherever that relation has been introduced, it has been followed and regulated, in the absence of other legislation, by the principles of the Roman law.

251. In concluding this slight sketch relative to the history of the Roman law, since the time of Justinian, some notice will now be taken, first, of the glossators; second, of certain of the great writers on the Roman law, since the glossators; and thirdly, of what is called the German historical school.

SECTION I.— *The Glossators.*

252. Irnerius, who was one of the first professors in the school of Bologna, illustrated the text of Justinian's compilations by brief notes, which were called *glosses*. At first these notes were inserted in the text, with the words to which they referred (*glossæ interlineares*); but, afterwards, they were placed in the margin, partly at the side, and partly under the text (*glossæ marginales*). Irnerius was followed by other professors and jurists, in this method of annotation; whose notes were at length collected together and compiled into one by Accursius, about the middle of the thirteenth century. The work of Accursius, in which he inserted many notes of his own, was called the *Glossa Ordinaria*. It was afterwards enlarged by additions from the writings of the later jurists.

253. The gloss of Accursius enjoyed a very great authority; so much, indeed, that it was considered of more weight than the text itself. But, it was not the work of men either of genius or of learning, though, occasionally, manifesting great sagacity; and it is chiefly remarkable as the production of the first century of the scientific renovation of the Roman law. The gloss is also the test, by which to determine, in general, what parts of the works of

Justinian are admitted as law in Germany. The reason is, that the glossed parts only are considered as applicable, and not because any more authority is attributed to the gloss itself, than to the notes of other commentators: *Quicquid glossa non agnoscit, illud nec agnoscit curia.* The glossed parts of the Corpus Juris Civilis are the institutes, digest, code, and ninety-seven of the novels; but in these there are several unglossed passages.

Section II.— *Cujas, Domat, Heineccius, Pothier.*

254. Of the immense number of writers, of every description, who have commented upon, or treated in some way of, the Roman law, it is proposed to mention only four, namely, Cujas, Domat, Heineccius, and Pothier; not because these are the most worthy to be spoken of, though the first named is called by his countrymen, the great Cujas; but, because, as their works are much in use in this country, some knowledge of these authors, the three last especially, will be most useful to us.

255. Cujas, who was born at Toulouse, in 1520, and died in 1590, seems to have been the first who became sufficiently aware of the importance and value of the sources of the law anterior to the time of Justinian, for explaining the Corpus Juris Civilis. He therefore collected a great number of manuscripts, which he made use of, both for this purpose

and for that of correcting the text of the law. In order to get at the exact meaning of the writings in the digest, his method was to collect the different fragments and detached sentences of the same author upon a particular subject together; and to restore the ancient and original arrangement.

256. Domat, who was born at Clermont, in Auvergne, in 1625, and died in 1695, besides being the author of a *Legum Delectus*, and a treatise on public law, compiled a work entitled the civil laws in their natural order, which, with the treatise on public law, has been translated into English by Dr. Strahan. This latter work is one of the most useful works on the Roman law in the English language.[1]

257. Heineccius, who was born at Lubec, in 1680, and died in 1741, was the first law professor and writer of his time. He wrote several treatises on the Roman law, and especially two, in the form of elements, one according to the order of the pandects, and the other according to the order of the institutes. His method of treating the subject in these works, is the axiomatic method, in which the process consists in deriving one axiom from another. The elements of Heineccius enjoyed a great celebrity, and have within a few years been edited and republished. They are frequently met with in our libraries, and have been much admired. It is said, that his me-

---

1 A new edition of this translation, under the editorial supervision of the author of the present book, was recently published in Boston, by Messrs. Little, Brown & Co. in two volumes, royal 8vo.

thod of teaching, by axioms, savors too much of the scholastic logic; but, on the other hand, Sir James Mackintosh pronounces him to be "the best writer of elementary books," with whom he is acquainted, on any subject.

258. Pothier, who was born at Orleans, in 1699, and died in 1772, is perhaps better known to English and American lawyers than almost any other writer on the Roman law. His great work on the pandects is a monument of laborious diligence. His method is quite different from that of Cujas. Pothier adopted the general plan of the books and titles of Justinian, but changed the order of the excerpts or fragments contained in them. He divided and subdivided the fragments, and distributed them throughout the various titles, for the purpose of obtaining a more scientific arrangement, and bringing together the different passages relating to each particular point.

259. This work is not confined to the texts of the pandects, although it contains them all. Pothier introduces, also, the imperial constitutions, where the law of the pandects has been changed by them; and the whole is connected together by language of his own. The two last titles (the 16th and 17th) of the fiftieth book, concerning the signification of words and divers rules of the ancient law, have been very much enlarged and expanded by Pothier. The last, especially, constitutes a complete treatise of itself, and may be considered as an epitome of the whole Roman law, in the form of maxims and principles.

260. Pothier prefixed to this work:—I. A historical preface;—II. The fragments of the laws of the twelve tables, as they are collected and arranged by Jacques Godefroi, with a commentary and notes, and also an appendix containing the fragments attributed to the twelve tables by other writers, explained in the same manner;—III. The fragments of the perpetual edict arranged in the order of the digest, with notes;—IV. A list of the authors cited by the compiler, both in the text and the notes.

261. The preface is divided into three parts. The first gives an account of the sources from which the Roman law has been derived, and of the different parts of which it is composed. The second contains an interesting biography of the jurisconsults, whose writings were employed in the compilation of the digest, or whose opinions are therein quoted. These jurisconsults, as has already been stated, were divided into two principal sects,[1] who embraced and promulgated opposite opinions upon certain questions. These opinions, being sometimes introduced into the digest, constitute what are called antinomies. They have heretofore been adverted to and explained, and examples of them given. The third part of the preface is devoted to an account of the composition of the several parts of Justinian's compilations; of the degree of authority enjoyed by that collection; of its destiny, upon the decline, and after the fall, of

---

[1] See *ante*, 183.

the empire, until the revival of letters, and the reëstablishment of the schools of law.

262. This work earned for its author, with the greater part of the French jurists, the title of *Pandectarum Restitutor Felicissimus;* and "such is its value," says Pothier's biographer and editor,[1] "that, in my opinion, if it were necessary to choose between its loss, and that of all the other works composed upon the Roman law, I should not hesitate to exclaim, 'Save the pandects of Pothier.'" Without subscribing entirely to this eulogium, or assenting to the justice of the remark, on the other hand, that a principal merit of Pothier's work has been to prevent the Roman law from falling into oblivion, in France, after the introduction of the new codes, the belief, formerly expressed,[2] may be repeated, that, in the present state of the study and knowledge of the Roman law in this country, the American lawyer will find the pandects of Pothier more useful and convenient, in practice, and for ordinary consultation, than the Corpus Juris Civilis, with all its attendant army of commentators and its advance guard of institutists, epitomists, and abbreviators.

263. Besides this work on the pandects, Pothier composed numerous treatises on French law, in which the leading principles are drawn from the Roman law. These works may be divided into two classes, those which are founded in French customs

---

[1] M. Dupin.

[2] American Jurist, XII. 372.

and usages, to which the Roman law is merely accessory, and those which are founded in Roman law, to which the French law is merely accessory. The treatises on the customary law are of the former class; those on obligations and contracts, of the latter.

264. The treatise on obligations is a full, methodical, and admirably arranged work on the whole subject of which it treats. The author, in this work, considers agreements in themselves, in their elementary formation, in their essence, in their different modalities, in their execution, and finally, in their dissolution; and in treating all these matters, he considers them, as he expresses it, according to the rules of the forum of conscience, as well as of the exterior forum.

265. This work is a repertory of the general principles, which are equally applicable under all systems, and to every particular form of contract, and which are carried out and exemplified by the author in his other works. Of this treatise, the editor of Pothier's works does not hesitate to say, that "it is the most perfect book of law that ever issued from the hand of man; and not only a good book of law, but an excellent book of morals; a work of all countries and of all nations; a book to which antiquity can present no rival but the *Offices of Cicero*, and which has no superior but the Gospel."[1]

---

[1] There are two translations of this celebrated work into English. The first was published at Newbern, North Carolina, in 1802, without the name of the translator, in one volume, 8vo, under the title of, *A Treatise on Obligations, considered in a moral and legal view.* This is

266. After thus treating of obligations in general, Pothier published a great number of treatises on particular contracts, in which the principles laid down in the former work are applied and exemplified. Those which relate to subjects or matters peculiar to the laws of France, though more or less connected with general jurisprudence, need not be enumerated. The others, which are not peculiar to the laws of France, but belong to every civilized country, such, for example, as the treatises on the contracts of sale, letting to hire, partnership, loan for use, or consumption, deposit, mandate, insurance, bottomry, deserve the most attentive consideration, and will richly reward the labor of the student of the common law.[1]

267. The testimony of Sir William Jones,[2] a competent judge both of the common and Roman law, to the extraordinary merit of these treatises, has been

---

supposed to be the production of Francois Xavier Martin, afterwards presiding judge of the Supreme Court of Louisiana. The other translation, which is the one in common use, by Sir William D. Evans, late recorder of Bombay, was first published at London, in 1806, with an introduction, appendix, and notes, in two volumes, 8vo. It has been more than once reprinted in this country, the last time in Philadelphia, in 1839.

The treatise on the contract of sale has been translated by the author of the present work; and a part of that on the contract of letting to hire, under the title of "A Treatise on Maritime Contracts of letting to hire," by the Hon. Caleb Cushing, now Attorney-General of the United States.

[1] For a full account of the life and writings of Pothier, see American Jurist, XII. 341.

[2] Essay on Bailments, 29.

often quoted:—"At the time when this author (Le Brun) wrote, the learned M. Pothier was composing some of his admirable treatises on all the different species of express or implied contracts; and here I seize with pleasure an opportunity of recommending those treatises to the English lawyer, exhorting him to read them again and again; for if his great master, Littleton, has given him, as it must be presumed, a taste for luminous method, apposite examples, and a clear, manly style, in which nothing is redundant, nothing deficient, he will surely be delighted with works in which all those advantages are combined, and the greatest portion of which is law at Westminster as well as at Orleans; for my own part, I am so charmed with them, that, if my undissembled fondness for the study of jurisprudence were never to produce any greater benefit to the public than barely the introduction of Pothier to the acquaintance of my countrymen, I should think that I had in some measure discharged the debt which every man, according to lord Coke, owes to his profession."

268. The works of Pothier have not, indeed, like the writings of the ancient Roman jurisconsults, been received as laws; but they have obtained an equivalent honor; since more than three fourths of the civil code (commonly called the *Code Napoleon*) have been literally extracted from his treatises. Of this fact any one may see evidence, by examining the third title of book third, concerning conventional obligations in general, which is nothing more than a

continued analysis of the treatise on obligations. Not only are the divisions of that work preserved, and the same principles established, (with the exception of four or five articles), but the very language of Pothier is employed. Thus, the nine rules given in the code for the interpretation of contracts, (articles 1156 to 1164, both inclusive), are the same with nine out of the twelve rules, laid down by Pothier for the same purpose.[1] There is a similar conformity in the titles of usufruct, habitation, possession, property, prescription, sale, letting to hire, and many others.

Section III. — *German Historical School.*

269. The German Historical School, as it is called, has had too important an influence upon the science to be omitted, even in the shortest sketch of Roman law. The origin of this celebrated school or sect, though the elements of it existed before, is as follows. The emperor Napoleon, having accomplished his great reform in French law, introduced his codes into those of the states of Germany which he succeeded in conquering; so, that, when he was himself defeated, and his power overthrown, the French codes were actually in force as law, in many parts of Bavaria, Hesse Darmstadt, the Rhenish provinces of

---

[1] Treatise on Obligations, 91, 92, 93, 94, 95, 97, 98, 100.

Prussia, the kingdom of Westphalia, Baden, the Hanseatic towns, and some of the other German Rhenish provinces. On the downfall of Napoleon, his codes were instantly abrogated in all the German states in which they had been established, with the exception of the Rhenish provinces. There the French codes were retained, and probably constitute the law at the present time.

270. In those states which had thus rejected the French codes, after living under them for some time, the question immediately arose, whether it would not be preferable to have a code of their own, rather than go back to the old mixed system of customary, Roman, canon, and German law, which had previously been in use. The first opinion was maintained by Thibaut, a celebrated member of the faculty of law at Heidelberg, in a tract entitled, *On the necessity of a general Civil Law for Germany*, in which he advocated the adoption of measures for the preparation of a code for the whole of Germany. This proposition was opposed by Savigny, a celebrated law professor of Berlin, in a pamphlet entitled, *On the Vocation of the present Age for Legislation and Jurisprudence*, in which he deprecated the adoption of the scheme recommended by Thibaut, as hazardous, and maintained the expediency of reverting to the system which had been superseded by the French. Other writers succeeded, on both sides, until, at length, the German jurists seem to have become

pretty much divided on the great question of codification.

271. One of the leading arguments, urged by Savigny and his followers, was the then state of the law as a science. They maintained, that the Roman law, as it was known and taught at the time, was not in a fit condition to be embodied and fixed in an irrevocable form; that, upon many points, the commonly received doctrine was obscure and imperfect; that a further study of the sources would be necessary to ascertain the true doctrine; and finally, that the mode proposed, that is, the making of a code, was not the true mode of legislating for a country; which should be left to the more gradual improvement and extension of the jurists and the courts.

272. These positions were enforced with great learning and ability by Savigny, in the tract referred to, and were strengthened by several very apposite illustrations drawn by him from the French codes; in which it was entirely manifest, that the compilers, intending to pursue and adopt the Roman law, had, in fact, totally misconceived it, and had consequently introduced something else into their codes. In short, it would not, perhaps, be too much to say, that the anticodifiers would have preferred to go back to the old Roman system of the prætor's edict, the *responsa prudentium*, and the commentaries of the lawyers.

273. It will be perceived, by this sketch of the code controversy, that Savigny and his followers, in studying the science of law, whether Roman or other, would pursue it historically; that is, they would trace back every institution to its origin, and then follow it down through all the changes which it might have undergone, and thus ascertain its precise meaning and extent. The investigation of the Roman law, on this plan, would also require the possession of all that could be obtained of the sources from whence Justinian had drawn his compilations, or which were in existence at the time they were made, or which could in any manner serve to explain and illustrate the origin or meaning of the legal institutions of the Romans.

274. The publication of Savigny's work brought out and developed this method, and induced those who agreed with him in his opinion of codification, to engage in investigations which had the history of the law more or less for their object; and hence originated a class of writers, who, without any other bond of union than this common method and purpose, were denominated the German historical school, and who exercised, and probably still exercise, a great influence upon the study of the law on the continent of Europe.

275. The code controversy, turned in this direction, gave a most extraordinary impulse to the study of the Roman law in Germany, on the historical method; which has thrown great light on many

controverted points, as well as on the general subject, and has led to a more accurate apprehension of the meaning and extent of many of the established doctrines of the law. A further impulse to this study was also given by the discovery of the original commentaries of Gaius, and of some other original sources of the Roman law, very soon after the publication of Savigny's tract on codification.

276. The labors of these writers it is impossible here to describe; or even to mention their names. It would be no more than just, perhaps, to say of them, that, if a knowledge of the laws of any country, and of the sources of those laws, can ever be carried to such a degree of perfection, as to justify the reducing of them into the form of a code, the Roman and other sources of law in Germany have been brought by them into, and are unquestionably in, a proper condition to be codified at the present moment.

277. The study of the Roman law, however, in Germany, has not been confined to the writers of the historical school; nor has it been taught wholly according to the historical method. Works of a different description have been equally abundant, and the science has been taught dogmatically as well as historically. In Mackeldy's work,[1] which the American translator and editor of it entitles a "Compendium of Modern Civil Law," both methods

---

[1] Lehrbuch des heutigen Ræmischen Recht. See *ante*, 224.

have been apparently used. The author avails himself of all the light, which the labors of the historical school have thrown on the subject, and at the same time explains the law precisely as it is.[1]

278. The question of codification, which first gave an impulse to the historical school, seems either to have been given up, or to have taken a subordinate position; at all events, the project of a general code for all Germany was abandoned. But, notwithstanding the opposition which this plan encountered, and which seems to have prevailed, a great many codes of criminal law have been framed for the different German states, and have been successfully put in operation. The codification of the civil law has not, probably, been carried much if any further than when Savigny wrote. There were then three general codes in existence, the French, Prussian, and Austrian.

279. The labors of the historical school have established an entirely new and distinct era in the study of the Roman jurisprudence; and though these writers cannot be said to have thrown their predecessors into the shade, it seems to be generally admitted, that almost every branch of the Roman law has received some important modification at their hands, and that a knowledge of their writings, to some extent,

---

[1] This work, in the above-mentioned translation, may be recommended, on the whole, as the best, for the purposes of an introduction to the Roman law, which is within the reach of the American student.

at least, is essentially necessary to its acquisition. In referring, therefore, to writers of an older date than the present century, (for the labors of some eminent writers were turned in the historical direction as early as its commencement), and in making use of their writings, it will certainly be no more than a prudent precaution, at the same time, to consult some more modern general treatise, like that, for example, of Mackeldy.[1]

---

[1] For a full account of the German Historical School, see American Jurist, XIV. 43.

CHAPTER VIII.

CONTENTS OF JUSTINIAN'S COMPILATIONS AND MODE OF REFERRING TO THEM.

280. The compilations executed by the orders of Justinian, namely, the institutes, digest, code, and novels, are most commonly embraced in one volume, and published under the name of the Corpus Juris Civilis; in which form they were first collected together, about the end of the twelfth, and first published under that title in the sixteenth,[1] century. They have, however, been published separately, especially the institutes, which exist in a great variety of forms.

281. But in almost all the editions of the Corpus Juris Civilis, of which there is quite a number, we find, besides the works above enumerated, several other documents which are entirely foreign to the Roman law, and have nothing to do with the labors of Justinian. These are certain constitutions of divers of the eastern emperors; the *Canones Sanctorum;* the *Libri Feudorum;* certain constitutions of Frederic II. and Henry VII., emperors of Germany;

---

[1] Themis X. 283.

the treaty of peace (*Liber de pace Constanciæ*) concluded between Frederic I. and certain confederated cities of Lombardy. These supplements were originally inserted in the Corpus Juris Civilis, on account of their convenience, in ancient times, in practice; they are of no use at the present day.

282. Some account will now be given of the different methods of referring to or citing the several works constituting the compilations of Justinian, as they exist in the Corpus Juris Civilis. The number of treatises of various kinds, in which these works are referred to, being very great, and some of them in daily use, it will be found quite essential, in pursuing the study of the Roman law, or in making use of it in practice, to become acquainted with the various methods of citing it, which have prevailed at different times, or been adopted by different authors.

283. The institutes are divided into four books, each of which is divided into titles, which are severally subdivided into sections or paragraphs. The digest is divided into fifty books, each book into titles, each title into laws, (sometimes also called fragments), and many of the laws into sections or paragraphs. Books 30, 31, and 32, which treat of legacies and trusts, are not divided into several titles, but contain each of them a single title only, with the same rubric,[1] namely, *de legatis et fideicommissis.*

---

[1] The titles, or inscriptions of the titles, derive this appellation from the fact, that they were at first written in red letters.

The code is divided into twelve books, each book into titles, each title into laws, and the laws frequently into paragraphs or sections, in the same manner with the digest. The novels, or new constitutions, are each numbered, and divided into chapters. The several books, titles, laws, and paragraphs, in each of the different parts of which the Corpus Juris Civilis is composed, are numbered consecutively. The titles only have a rubric.

284. There are, in general, two principal modes by which, in works of this description, we may indicate what passages we refer to, namely, by means of words, and by means of figures; using for the first, the rubrics of the titles or the first words of the excerpts, and for the last, the numbers denoting the book, title, law, and paragraph.[1]

285. The first has the advantage, that it is not so difficult to recollect words as numbers; that as the number must also be expressed, when the quotation is oral, the numerical order is not unfrequently longer and more compounded than other words, by which the passage may be known, as, for example, *lex vicesima octava*, the number of a particular law, is longer than *lex si contendat*, its initial words; that in speech, or otherwise, when the book itself is at hand, other persons will more readily call to mind the pas-

[1] In what follows, I have availed myself, to some extent, of an article in the American Jurist, XV. 63, translated from Hugo's Civilistisches Magazin, IV. 212, and from Berriat-Saint-Prix's History of the Roman law, section iv. chap. vii.

sage referred to, if it is described to them by itself, that is, by its title or by its initial words, than by the mere indication, in numbers, of the place where it is to be found ; and, lastly, that confusion is not so likely to occur from the use of words, as from that of several independent numbers indicating the book, title, law, and paragraph.

286. On the other hand, where references or citations are made in writing or printing, the numerical order of the different passages is manifestly the shortest; and it is also much easier to look for a text by its number than by its description or initial words.

287. It follows, consequently, that words are more proper for oral, and numbers for writtten or printed, citations ; and also, that the former are more convenient for those who are familiarly acquainted with the book referred to, and the latter for those who are not so.

288. According to the first of these fundamental principles, the ancient jurists, whose works were used in the composition of the digest, referred to the writings of one another, by means of numbers. The inscriptions of the laws or fragments excerpted in the digest are arranged, throughout, upon this mode of citation. In the novels, Justinian refers to his compilations according to the number of the books. Theophilus,[1] in his paraphrase of the institutes, cites

[1] Soon after the publication of the institutes, Theophilus, a professor of law at Constantinople, delivered lectures, in Greek, on the principles

according to the number of the book and of the title. In the Basilica,[1] the references are made in the same manner, with the addition of the number of the passage; and this is also the case with the later Greek jurists.

289. But in the time of Irnerius, and in that immediately succeeding, that is, during the period of the glossators, when the oral delivery of lectures came into vogue; when the custom of disputation prevailed, in which a principal part of the instruction, in regard both to the teacher and pupil, consisted; and when the advocates, in their oral conflicts at the bar, were accustomed to appeal to the authority of particular passages; it became more natural, instead of citing the texts referred to by their number, to cite them by their initial words, or by the inscriptions or rubrics of the titles, with an indication of the compilation referred to.

290. To facilitate this mode of citation, some of the earlier editions of the Corpus Juris contain a table or register of the laws, arranged in alphabetical order, according to their initial words. The contrivance of the juridical playing-cards, by means of which the laws *quoad verba initialia*, might be learned by heart, is to be attributed to the same

---

contained in that work. The commentary of this professor, which has come down to modern times, is known by the name of the Greek paraphrase of the institutes.

[1] See *ante*, ~~290.~~ 241.

cause.[1] This mode of citing prevailed among the glossators and other early writers on the Roman law, and some traces of it still remain.[2]

291. While this method of citing was in use, it was not customary to add any number to the initial words, except when several other passages commenced with the same words; in which case the number of the passage beginning with the same words, and not the number of the passage generally, was added. Thus, for example, in the title *quod metus causa*, which is the second title of the fourth book of the digest, the third of the passages which begin with the word *metum* is, in connection with the other laws of this title, the ninth. Hence, it was for a long time cited as the *lex metum*, 3, *D. quod metus causa.* Afterwards, it was cited as the *lex metum* 3. Finally, the initial words were dispensed with altogether, and the passage was cited merely

---

[1] To this mode of citing, also, is to be referred the not unaptly imagined citation in Racine's *Plaideurs*, where the advocate of the dog, who had been dragged from his kennel, for having eaten a capon, says:—

> Qui ne sait, que la loi *si quis canis*, Digeste,
> *De vi*, paragraphe, messieurs, *caponibus*, *etc.*

[2] In the early ages, an indication of the numbers of the titles would not have been useful, any more than that of the numbers of the laws, because they were not the same in all the editions; but with the publication of the edition of Dionysius Gothofredus (or, Denys Godefroi.) which was generally received at the bar, the numbering of the titles and laws appears to have become uniform.

as *lex* 3. So the laws 1, 58, 63, 67, of the third title of the third book of the digest, *de procuratoribus et defensoribus*, begin by the same word *procurator.* The law 63 was consequently cited as *l. procurator* 3, *ff*, *de procuratorib.*, because it is the third of the same title which begins with the word *procurator.*

292. The invention of printing, which, in general, gave to instruction out of books a great preponderance over the oral method by lectures; which, also, made a more frequent revision and correction of the numbers possible, and consequently secured a much greater degree of accuracy in the use of them; and which, besides, very much enlarged the reading and knowledge of the jurists, hitherto confined within the limited circle of juridical books, made the method of citing by numbers more appropriate and necessary, as well as less liable to mistake, than before.

293. The use of printing, however, was not followed at once by the substitution of numbers for initial words in citing. Instead of this, the custom grew up by degrees, especially in Germany, of adding the number to the initial words, which, as already remarked, had only been practised when several other passages commenced with the same words.

294. At length, the old method of citing appears to have been superseded, to a great extent, if not entirely, by a combination of words and figures;

the former (preceded by the initial letter of the compilation referred to) to denote the title, in which the passage cited occurs, and the latter the number which it bears in that title. This system, which is adopted by the authors, to whose works we have most frequent occasion to resort, among others by Domat and Pothier, requires to be explained at some length.

295. The digest is denoted by the letter *D.* or the sign *ff*[1]; the institutes, by the letter *I.*, or the abbreviation *Inst.;* the code, by the letter *C.*, or *Cod.;* the novels, by the letter *N.*, or *Nov.* The letter *L.* or *l.* is used to designate a law, both in the code as well as the digest; the sign §, a paragraph or section of a law of the code or digest, or of a title of the institutes.

296. The general plan of reference to the institutes, digest, and code, is by the rubric of the title, or, where the rubric is long, by the first two or three words of it, with the number of the law, and also of the paragraph where the law cited is thus divided. The words of the title are usually abbreviated.

---

[1] Sometimes, and particularly in the works of the earlier writers, instead of the letter *D.* the sign *ff* is used to denote the digest. This sign is nothing more than the letter *D.* somewhat distorted in writing, with a line drawn across it, to indicate that it is an abbreviation, and, which, not being understood by the more recent copyists and editors, has been gradually transformed into *ff.* See American Jurist, XV. 79, note. See, also, Themis, V. 47, 115.

297. Where several titles of the part cited have the same first word or words, we use several of these words, until we come to where the two titles begin to differ. If we wish, for example, to cite the title of the digest, *de his qui effuderint vel dejecerint*, and the title *de his qui notantur infamia*, we say, for the first, *D. de his qui effuder.*, and for the second, *D. de his qui notant.*

298. When a citation refers to one of the titles which are most used, the initial letters only, put in capitals, are employed. This is the case with the following, among other titles, namely, *de verborum significatione*, *de regulis juris*, *de verborum obligationibus*, *de obligationibus et actionibus*, *de justitia et jure*, which are designated, the first by *V. S.*, the second by *R. J.*, the third by *V. O.*, the fourth by *O. et A.*, and the fifth by *J. et J.* Thus, *l.* 2, *D. R. J.* designates the second law in the title of the digest, *de regulis juris.*

299. With these remarks the mode of reference will best be farther explained by examples: —

L. 2, *D. de fidej. et mand.* — This reference denotes the second law of the title of the digest *de fidejussoribus et mandatoribus*, which will be found, by reference to the subjoined table, to be the first title of the forty-sixth book.

L. 29, § 6, *D. mand.* — This refers to the sixth section or paragraph of the twenty-ninth law of the title of the digest *mandati vel contra*, which is the first title of the seventeenth book.

L. 10, § *ult. D. mand.*— The last paragraph of the tenth law of the same title of the digest.

L. 1, *C. de fidej. min.*— The first law of the title of the code *de fidejussoribus minorum*, which is the twenty-fourth title of the second book.

§ 1, *Inst. de duob. reis.*— Institutes, the first paragraph of the title *de duobus reis stipulandi et promittendi*, which is the sixteenth title of the third book.

L. pen. C. de non num. pec.— The last law but one of the title of the code *de non numerata pecunia*, which is the thirtieth title of the fourth book.

300. The abbreviation *eod.* denotes the title given in the reference next immediately preceding: thus, *L.* 9, § *ult. eod.*, immediately following the reference *L.* 20, § 2, *D. de pign. act.*, denotes the last paragraph of the ninth law of the title of the digest *de pignoratitia actione vel contra*, which is the seventh title of the thirteenth book.

301. If the last reference be to a different part of the Corpus Juris Civilis from the first, the part referred to is designated by the proper letter or abbreviation: thus, *L. ult. Cod. eod.*, following immediately after *L.* 4, *D. in quib. caus. pign. vel hyp. tac. contr.*, which is the second title of the twentieth book of the digest, denotes the last law of the code contained in the title bearing the same rubric with the title of the digest referred to, namely, the fifteenth title of the eighth book, *in quibus causis pignus vel hypotheca tacite contrahitur*.

302. The words *in fine*, or the abbreviations *in fin.*,

in f., denote that the particular passage referred to is *at the end* of the law or paragraph thus designated.

303. The letters *D. l.* denote the *said law*, that is, the law designated by the reference next immediately preceding. *D. ll.* are used when more than one law is referred to. *D. t.*, the *said title*. *D.* §, the *said section* or *paragraph*.

304. Some of the titles contain but a single law. When this is the case, the reference is in this form: *L. un.* (*unica*) *C. ut caus. post pubert. ads. tut.*, or the only law in the title of the code *ut causæ post pubertatem adsit tutor*, which is the forty-eighth title of the fifth book.

305. The words *in principio*, or the abbreviations *in pr.*, denote the *beginning* of the law, or of the other particular part referred to. Where a law is divided into several paragraphs, the first is not numbered, and is referred to in this manner. Thus, by *L.* 1, *in prin. D. de calumniat.*, is meant the paragraph at the beginning of the first law of the title of the digest *de calumniatoribus*, which is the sixth title of the third book. *L.* 71, *in f. princ. D. de fidej. et mand.* At the end of the paragraph commencing the law seventy-first, &c.

306. The letter *V.*, as *V. l.* 1, § 3, &c. (that is, *see* the passage referred to), indicates that the law designated is referred to, not as directly, but only by analogy, or indirectly, supporting the principle or proposition to which it is cited.

307. The same thing, nearly, is indicated by the sign *arg.*, as, for example, *arg. l.* 35, *quod sæpe*, &c., by which it is signified, that the writer argues from the law thus referred to in favor of his proposition.

308. *L. un.* (*unica*) § 7, *versic.* (*versiculus*) *sin autem*, *cod. de rei ux. act.* This refers to the seventh paragraph of the only law of the code, book fifth, title thirteen, *de rei uxoriæ actione*, &c., at the sentence commencing with the words *sin autem.*

309. The three books, 30, 31 and 32 of the digest, which treat of legacies and trusts, and each of which contains but a single title, with the same rubric, *de legatis et fideicommissis*, are referred to as *de legat.* 1, *de legat.* 2, *de legat.* 3. Thus, *L.* 37, § 5, *D. de legat.* 3, denotes the digest, book thirty-second, law 37, § 5.[1]

310. Sometimes a text is referred to both by its initial words and by its number, as, for example, *l. quod sæpe*, 35, § *in his* 5, *D. contrah. emt.*, by which is designated the fifth paragraph or section of the thirty-fifth law of the first title of the eighteenth book of the digest.[2]

---

1 These three books, in fact, constitute but one, divided into three parts, of a convenient size, probably, for being written on parchment. If compiled at the present day, for the purpose of being printed, they would, doubtless, be included in a single volume, with one title only, Legacies and Trusts. See *post*, 320.

2 When there is occasion to discuss the terms or the applicability of a particular passage, or otherwise to mention it, we denote it not unfrequently by the initial words, precisely as in discussing a point of

311. The jurists, whose writings were excerpted in the digest, were at the same time authorized expounders of law, advisers in legislation, and writers of law treatises. Before this time, these writings were included under the term *jus*. When inserted in the digest, they became *lex*, that is, the whole mass of excerpts contained in the digest, by receiving the emperor's confirmation, became a work of legislation. Hence it has been usual to call the several passages excerpted, *leges*. But though the whole compilation obtained the force of law, the term laws is not strictly applicable to the several excerpts, taken individually.[1]

312. It is clearly improper, as Hugo observes, to call the second excerpt in the ninth title of the forty-seventh book of the digest, which consists merely of the words *et loco*, a law; or to give that appellation to the historical fact:—*Partus pignoratæ ancillæ in pari causa esse, qua mater est, olim placuit*, which constitutes the whole of the first excerpt in the twenty-fifth title of the eighth book of the code.

313. For this reason, and also because these individual excerpts, of which the digest is composed,

---

the common law, relating to estates tail, we speak of the statute *de donis conditionalibus*. Thus, writers on the Roman law, on the subject of responsibility for neglect, (Jones on Bailments, 22,) speak of the law *Si ut certo* (*D.* 13, 6, 5), and the law *Contractus* (*D.* 50, 17, 23). So Pothier, in his General Observation, alludes to the latter as the famous law *Contractus*.

[1] Long, Discourses, 76, and note.

are, in reality, nothing but extracts or fragments taken from the private law writers before the time of Justinian, they are sometimes cited, particularly by the modern German writers, as *fragments*, (designated by the abbreviation *fr.*), either with or without the author's name. Thus, the sixteenth excerpt, in the second title of the thirty-third book of the digest, is taken from the responses of Modestinus, one of the writers, whose works were used in the compilation of the digest, and is entitled:— *Modestinus, libro* IX. *Responsorum.* This text is referred to, in the manner above indicated, as *Modest. fr.* 16, *de usu, et usufr.*

314. But the passages in the code are not fragments, and many of them at least have never been any larger than they now are. The word *fragment*, therefore, is no more appropriate than the word law, to designate them. A better term than either is the word *constitutio* (abbreviated *c.*, *co.*, or *const.*), which is sometimes used. "But," as is remarked by Berriat-Saint-Prix, though "the term *law* is certainly not the most proper to designate these texts, it has been in some sort legitimated, for several centuries, by the usage of all the authors, even those of the first rank."

315. The ancient writers, as well as the more modern authors, cite the *novels* by the first words of the rubric, frequently with the addition of the number of the collation, as well as the title and chapter. Thus, where they referred to the third chapter of

novel 118, relative to collateral succession, they wrote *Auth.* (the novels are also denominated *authentics*) *de heredib. ab intest. c.* 3, *collat.* 9, *tit.* 1. But this is a somewhat uncertain designation. There are many editions of the Corpus Juris, which have no one hundred and eighteenth novel, and there are many, also, in which the one hundred and eighteenth does not relate to the subject of succession. The novels are now commonly referred to by their numbers, which are not the same in the older editions, and the number of the chapter.

316. The *authentics of the code* are cited only by their first words, preceded by the sign *Auth.* and followed by an indication of the title and law of the code in which they are inserted, as follows: — *Auth. si qua mulier, C, ad S. C. Velleianum.* This reference denotes the authentic appended to the twenty-second law of the twenty-ninth title of the fourth book of the code.

317. A third mode of citing, which is the most common at the present day, consists in the use of numbers only. It appears to have been first introduced by Ayliffe, an English author, who published, in 1734, the first volume of *A new Pandect of Roman Civil Law*, with a preliminary discourse touching the rise and progress of the civil law.[1] In this work, he merely mentions in what part of the Corpus Juris the passage referred to is, and then gives

---

[1] This work was not completed.

the numbers which describe its locality, as, for example, *D.* 1, 2, 2, 5. The letter indicates the digest. The first number indicates the book, the second the title, the third the excerpt, and the fourth the paragraph. This method has been substantially followed by Gibbon, in his history, with the addition of abbreviations indicating the book and title to which the numbers respectively belong.

318. One of the advantages of this mode of citing, besides its greater facility, is, that it enables us to avoid confounding the digest and code, which, at least, in regard to the inscriptions that are common to both, often proves a source of confusion. When the number of the book cited exceeds 12, it is not in the code; and when the number of the title cited, in any one of the first twelve books, exceeds 22, or 15, in the first two books, or only exceeds 9 in any of the ten following, it does not belong to the pandects. In about 1200 titles, there are probably 100, in which it is as possible, that the book and title of the pandects are meant, as the book and title of the code; but, in all the others, and, consequently, in the proportion of 11 to 1, it is certain, that, according to the number, the title referred to is in the code alone, or in the pandects alone; for example, if the reference be 1, 5, or 2, 10, or 3, 4, &c., the work, (namely, the code or pandects) ought also to be mentioned; but, on the contrary, if it be 13, 1, or 20, 1, the work must necessarily be the pandects; or, if the reference be 1, 30, or 6, 60, it must be the code.

319. There are other modes of citation, which have been adopted and used by particular authors. They may all be readily resolved into the elements which are enumerated as constituting the three modes of citing above described, and do not require any distinct explanation.

320. The division of the institutes, digest, and code, into books, seems to have been made for those mere purposes of convenience, which are effected in modern times, since the invention of printing, by dividing a work into volumes. This is manifest for two reasons; first, the several books have no titles; and second, books 30, 31, and 32, embrace but a single topic, *legacies* and *trusts*, which are treated together, and have nominally each a title, *de legatis et fideicommissis;* and, if the division into books had been made by subjects, these three would have formed one book. The order and arrangement, therefore, are not to be determined by reference to the books, any more than, in modern times, the order and arrangement of a treatise would be determined by the distribution of the matter into volumes.

321. There seems to be about as much uniformity in the size of the books, as there is now in the size of volumes. The institutes and digest, with what precedes the latter, counted as one, contain fifty-five books. Reckoning the quantity of matter in them by the space they respectively occupy in Beck's edition, in octavo, of the Corpus Juris Civilis, the

average number of pages of each is thirty-nine and a half. The shortest book, (the twenty-fifth of the digest), contains only sixteen pages. One (the sixth) contains only nineteen. Fourteen books contain from twenty to thirty pages; sixteen from thirty to forty; fourteen from forty to fifty; six from fifty to sixty; there is one of sixty-one; and three over seventy. The largest book contains seventy-eight pages. Books 30, 31, and 32, would together make ninety-six pages. The books of the code appear to be much larger on an average than those of the digest. But it is not, perhaps, easy, from the space they occupy in the printed volume, to compare them with those of the digest.

322. The pandects were compiled in the same order with the perpetual edict. The fifty books, of which they are composed, were divided into seven parts, for no other reason, it seems, than the excellence of the number seven. The first is called *prota* (τά πρῶτα), either because it contains the general principles, or merely because it precedes the others; it comprehends the first four books. The second, which bears the same title as the fifth book, with which it begins, *de judiciis*, contains also the actions *in rem*, and divers detached titles; it extends to book eleventh. The third part, books twelve to nineteen, comprehends all contracts, except stipulations, and has received the name *de rebus* (*creditis*). The four last parts have not received from Justinian any particular names, and the commentators have

designated them sometimes by the rubric of their first title, sometimes under the generic name of *libri singulares*, because they each treated of divers detached matters. The fourth part, books twenty to twenty-seven,[1] treats of pledges and of hypothecations, interest, proofs, dowries, and nuptials, and guardianship. The fifth, books twenty-eight to thirty-six, treats of testaments, legacies, and trusts. The sixth part, books thirty-seven to forty-four, treats of the possession of goods, of the rights of patronage, of lawful inheritances, of donations, of enfranchisements, of interdicts, of exceptions, and of several other matters; it is terminated by the general title *de obligationibus et actionibus*. The seventh part, books forty-five to fifty, comprehends stipulations, the modes of extinguishing obligations, criminal law, appeals, municipal law, and, finally, the two titles *de verborum significatione*, and *de regulis juris*, which refer to all the matters of law.[2]

323. The glossators divided the digest into three books, namely: *digestum vetus*, which terminated with the second title of book XXIV. *de divortiis; infortiatum*, commencing with the third title of book XXIV; *soluto matrimonio*, and terminating with book XXXVIII; *digestum novum*, containing the residue. The reasons of these indications, are

---

[1] Sometimes called *umbilicus*, from its being the middle.
[2] Giraud, Introd. Hist. 406.

given at length by Savigny,[1] but they are of little importance to us.[2]

324. In connection with the compilations of Justinian, it seems proper to mention the pandects of Pothier, which have been already alluded to,[3] which contain not only the precise texts of the digest, but also those of the code and novels, (sometimes condensed), which are the necessary complement of the former; thus embracing, in one arrangement, the whole body of the Roman law, as it has come down to us in the Corpus Juris Civilis. In the third and fourth editions of this celebrated work, one in quarto and the other in folio, both published at Paris in 1818, the texts of the digest and code inserted in it, as well as the texts of the ancient law, have been collated and verified by the best editions.

325. In this work the order and arrangement of the books and titles, adopted by Justinian in the digest, are preserved; and under them, by means of other divisions and sub-divisions of his own, Pothier distributes all the texts in an orderly and scientific method. At the end of each volume, there is a table of the books and titles contained in it, and of the laws in each in their numerical order, as they stand

---

[1] History of the Roman Law in the Middle Ages, vol. iii. § 160, and following.

[2] "These divisions are arbitrary and absurd, and have been completely neglected by the moderns." Giraud, Historical Introduction to Heineccius's Elements, 424.

[3] See *ante*, 259 to 262.

in the digest, designated by their initial words, and with references to the book, title, and number where they occur in Pothier's arrangement. By this means any text of the digest may be found in that work. These tables, with those contained in an analysis of the work, which will be mentioned in the next paragraph, will enable one to find in Pothier's arrangement, any text that may be referred to either in the institutes, digest, code, or novels.

326. This work has been translated into French,[1] and published, with the original text, in twenty-four volumes octavo. One of the translators[2] is also the author of an analysis of the work, in Latin and French, published in two volumes octavo, containing several tables, which are equally applicable to the original and the translation. The analysis is a condensed abridgment of all the *titles* contained in the pandects, arranged in alphabetical order, as they stand in the French translation.

327. It contains, also, six tables in Latin and French, alphabetically arranged: 1. A table of all the books and titles of the digest, with references to the volume and page of the analysis, and through that, to the book and title of the pandects, in which the subject of each is treated; 2. A table of all the titles

---

[1] By Breard-Neuville and Moreau de Montalin. The translation, though useful in many respects, cannot be relied on with entire confidence.

[2] Moreau de Montalin.

of the institutes, referring to the analysis and also to the pandects; 3. A table of the titles of the code, with references to the analysis, and also to those books and titles of the pandects into which they are incorporated; 4. A table of all the titles and chapters of the novels, with references to the book, title, &c. of the pandects, in which they are cited or employed; 5. A table of the titles of the constitutions of the emperor Leo, which are sometimes cited by Pothier; 6. A table of all the books and titles of Pothier's pandects, under each of which all the laws of the code and novels incorporated into them are arranged.

328. It should be remarked, that the analysis does not include the two last titles, namely, the sixteenth and seventeenth of book fifty, *de verborum significatione* and *de regulis juris*, which, from their nature, do not admit of being analyzed. Whatever other divisions the compiler resorts to, and they are of different kinds, as parts, sections, articles, &c., according to the subject-matter, he numbers the paragraphs or laws, in each title, consecutively, from the beginning to the end; so that in citing Pothier's pandects it is only necessary to mention the book, title, and paragraph by their numbers, as *Poth. Pand.* 35, 1, 10.

CHAPTER IX.

UTILITY OF THE STUDY OF THE ROMAN LAW.

329. In order to form an adequate idea of the benefit which we may derive from the study of the Roman law, it will be necessary, in the first place, to indicate, in general terms, the extent to which it has been introduced into, or rather, the agency it has had in the formation of, the common law of England. For this purpose, it is important to call to mind the distinction, already adverted to and explained, between legislation and jurisprudence; and also to advert to another distinction, somewhat connected with it, between what may be called the political and the jural[1] elements of the legal system of a state. The former is, for the most part, and generally, the product of direct legislation, in some form; the latter is usually, and in an equal degree, the growth of jurisprudence. The political element is peculiar to each particular state, though not necessarily confined to one; the jural is or may be common to seve-

[1] For the origin and use of this word, see Lieber's Political Ethics, I. 173, n. (1).

ral, though they may possess different political elements.[1]

330. Thus, in the legal system of Rome, the institutions of domestic slavery, of paternal power, of adoption and emancipation, with many others, were essentially political in their character, and peculiar to the Roman state; while, on the other hand, the laws which related to obligations and contracts, to sale and exchange, and other matters of a like nature, were almost wholly jural, or jurisprudential in their origin, and equally applicable to the systems of other communities. So, too, the rules by which the details of the politico-legal institutions, to which we have adverted, were regulated and governed, were, for the most part, jurisprudential in their origin and character. Thus, also, in more modern times, the feudal system constituted one of the political elements in the legal institutions of every state in which it prevailed.

331. "The history of all nations of the ancient world," observes Niebuhr,[2] "ends in that of Rome, and that of all modern nations has grown out of that of Rome." If this be true, then we may infer, with lord chief justice Holt,[3] that "as all governments are sprung out of the Roman empire, so the laws of

---

[1] The former corresponds very nearly to the *jus civile*, and the latter to the *jus gentium*, of the Romans.

[2] Niebuhr's Lectures, by Schmitz, I. 92.

[3] *Lane* v. *Cotton*, 12 Mod. 472, 482.

all nations are doubtless raised out of the ruins of the civil law." It will be found, consequently, that wherever and to whatever extent the political institutions of the Romans were introduced into the states of modern Europe, they were accompanied by the system of laws by which those institutions were respectively governed and regulated; and that in all the European states, what we have called the jural element was more or less adopted directly, as the only system of law in existence equally applicable to all states.

332. In England, fewer of the political elements of the Roman law were introduced than in the states of continental Europe; but the general jurisprudence of that system was introduced there and recognized, and its authority admitted, at the very earliest period to which the history of the law extends back. Of this there is abundant evidence in the legal treatises which have come down to us from that period.

333. In the reign of Henry II., Glanville, who occupied a judicial station, published his work on the laws and customs of England. In this treatise, though bearing so comprehensive a title, the author treats merely of the ancient actions, and of the forms of writs then in use. In the reign of Henry III., Bracton, who is supposed also to have occupied a judicial station, compiled and published his very extensive and complete work *de legibus et consuetudinibus Angliæ*, which was followed, in the succeeding reign, by the several treatises denominated

Fleta and the Mirror of Justices, and by those of Britton and Thornton; of all which, Bracton's treatise is, in the main, the groundwork. A reference to the works of Glanville and Bracton, and especially to that of the latter, (neither of whom professed to treat of any law then for the first time introduced, or to quote authorities not before referred to), plainly shows, as Mr. Spence remarks,[1] "that the doctrines of the Roman law had been largely resorted to in the king's court."[2]

334. Hence, lord Holt, for the reason above stated by him, quotes the Roman law in a case then under consideration, and adds: — "It must be owned that the principles of our law are borrowed from the civil law; therefore governed by the same reason in many things; and all this may be, though the common law be time out of mind."[3] Similar testimonies of other judges and law writers might be added; one only will be sufficient.

335. The author of a "New Institute of the Imperial or Civil Law,"[4] remarks in his preface: —

---

[1] Eq. Jur. of the Court of Chancery, I. 119, 122, 123.

[2] It is remarkable, that Bracton's treatise, though the only complete repository of the ancient jurisprudence, and the great source of the common law, has not been reprinted since 1640. A new edition, with a translation and notes, would doubtless throw great light on the history and antiquities, as well as the common law of England, and be as well worthy of the attention of the government of that country, as some of the large and expensive publications of the record commission.

[3] *Lane* v. *Cotton*, 12 Mod. 472, 482.

[4] Wood's Institutes, London, 1704.

"Upon a review, I think it may be maintained, that a great portion of the civil law is part of the law of England, and interwoven with it throughout." The intelligent student of the common law, who explores its sources by the aid of the Roman law, cannot fail to perceive in how many and what points the former is indebted to the latter, and wherein the two systems are identical.

336. The learned and elegant commentaries on the laws of England, by Blackstone, bear about the same relation to the vast collections of Viner, Comyns, and Bacon, that the institutes of Justinian do to his digest and code, and are arranged throughout upon the same general plan with the imperial elements. Blackstone divides his work into four parts or books, under which he treats comprehensively of the whole subject of the laws of England. In the first and second books, he considers the *rights* that are commanded, and in the third and fourth, the *wrongs* that are forbidden, by the laws of England. His first book is devoted to the rights of persons; the second to the rights of things; the third to private wrongs, that is, an infringement of particular rights, which concern individuals only; and the fourth to public wrongs, which being a breach of general and public rights, affect the whole community, and are denominated crimes and misdemeanors.

337. This division conforms to the definition, which he had previously given of municipal law, "a rule

of civil conduct, commanding what is right and prohibiting what is wrong." But the titles, by which he designated the first and second parts of the division, seem to be derived from the word *jus*, as used in the institutes, translated into the word *right*, with a somewhat different meaning.

338. In the institutes, the word *jus* is used to denote the whole body of law or right on a particular subject. Thus it is said:— *Omne autem jus, quo utimur, ad personas pertinet, vel ad res, vel ad actiones.*[1] "All right which we enjoy pertains either to persons or to things or to actions." But this is a somewhat more extended meaning than the word *right* properly bears in English; in which it is used to signify the faculty which one has, in common with others, by the general law, or the privilege which one has, in virtue of some special law, of doing or demanding something to be done. Hence the learned commentator uses the word right in the plural, in which it comes nearer to the meaning of the word *jus* as above used, and entitles his first and second books the *rights* of persons and things.

339. Three kinds of *jus*, in the sense indicated above, are spoken of by the compilers of the institutes:—*jus naturale*, *jus civile*, and *jus gentium*.

340. The first, *jus naturale*, or natural right, is described as that which nature teaches to all animals; which is not peculiar to man, but is common to all

---

[1] Inst. 1, 3, 12.

animated beings, whether inhabitants of the air, the earth, or the water. To this kind of natural right belong the conjunction of the sexes, which is denominated marriage, the procreation of children, and their education. In this sense, the term *natural*, as applied to right or law, is no longer used.

341. The *jus civile*, or civil right, is that which each community or people establishes for itself, which is peculiar to it, and is, as it were, proper to that particular community. In modern times, this term is used in various senses; as, to denote the whole body of law for the government of the inhabitants of a state among themselves; to distinguish that portion of the same which does not, from that which does, relate to crimes and punishments; to denote the whole body of the Roman law, as it has come down to us.

342. The *jus gentium* is defined to be that law which natural reason appoints for all men, and which is equally observed by all nations. It is called the *jus gentium*, (usually translated "law of nations"), because the use of it is common to all *gentes*, that is, stocks, clans, tribes, or people, living together in the social state, as an aggregate community. In modern times, the law of nations is that system founded partly in natural right, partly in usages, and partly in consent, by which the affairs of nations, as such, among themselves, are regulated. This is now more properly denominated *public international law*.

343. To the *jus gentium*, the Romans attributed almost all contracts, such as sale, letting to hire, partnership, deposit, *mutuum*, and others. This is what Pothier means by the terms *pure natural right*, (or *law*), in his general classification of contracts.[1] " A fifth division of contracts," he remarks, " is into those which are subjected by the civil right to certain rules, or to certain forms, and into those which are regulated by pure natural right."

344. Bearing in mind, therefore, that by the rights of persons and things, Blackstone means only to designate the law relating to those subjects, respectively, and that the division of the institutes into books was merely for convenience, and has nothing whatever to do with a scientific arrangement of the matter of the treatise; we shall find, on a comparison of the two works, that there is an exact correspondence between them, as to the order and treatment of their respective subjects. Thus, the introduction of Blackstone corresponds to the preface and the first and second titles of the first book of the institutes; the first book of the commentaries to the third and following remaining titles of the first book of Justinian; the second book of the commentaries to the titles embraced under the second and third books of the institutes; the third book of the commentaries

---

[1] Treatise on Obligations, 15.

to the fourth book of the institutes, except the last title; and the fourth book of the commentaries to the last title of the institutes.

345. The subjects, in reference to which the common law has borrowed and adopted the doctrines of the Roman law, are of much too great extent and too numerous to be pointed out here. An example or two of the indirect influence of the latter will not be uninteresting. A curious trace of this sort may be found in the resemblance, which the modern form of a recognizance, taken in court or before a magistrate, bears to the form of entering into a verbal contract, according to the ancient Roman law. In this form, which was called a stipulation, the party to whom the promise was made, called the stipulator, addressing the other, said:—"Do you promise to pay me ten *aurei?*" to which the other, called the promisor, answered:—"I promise." The contract was then complete. Anciently, it was requisite, to the formation of a verbal contract, that certain solemn words should be used. But a constitution of the emperor Leo subsequently provided, that the apprehension and consent of the parties, expressed in any form of words, should constitute a valid contract.

346. The form of a stipulation, however, in which the party to whom the promise is made dictates its terms, continued to be employed. This is the exact form, in which a recognizance is entered into at the present day. The terms of the recognizance, usu-

ally of considerable length, are stated to the recognizor, who signifies his assent thereto in a single word, or by a mere sign. A similar form is retained in the contract of marriage, in which the words of the promise are dictated by the clergyman or magistrate, before whom the contract is entered into.

347. In order to make that acquaintance with this system, which will suffice for us as students of the common law, whether our object be general jurisprudence, or whether we have respect to those states, whose laws are founded upon the Roman, it will be expedient in the first place, to give the institutes an attentive and thorough perusal. Having accomplished this, the study of particular doctrines and titles may be carried further, to any desirable extent, by resorting to the other parts of Justinian's collections, or to works professedly treating of the subject particularly in view. The reading of the institutes ought to be preceded by that of some introductory work on the study of the Roman law.[1]

348. The student will also find it useful, either by way of introduction, or in connection with the institutes, to read the forty-fourth chapter of Gib-

---

[1] There is none in the English language that leaves nothing to be desired. The best that can be recommended is, perhaps, the translation of Mackeldy's treatise, by Kauffman, already referred to. See *ante*, 277.

bon's history, especially in the last edition, by Milman, which the editor has enriched with valuable and instructive notes. This chapter is received as a text book in some of the German universities. An edition of it in French was published at Liege, in 1821, with notes by professor Warnkoenig, which are almost all inserted in the edition above indicated. Long's Discourses,[1] in which the researches of the modern German jurists are turned to account, may be read with great profit. But the best work, introductory to the study of the Roman law, which the writer has ever seen, is the historical introduction to Heineccius's elements of Roman law, by M. Charles Giraud (in French), published at Paris, in 1838, as a separate work. An exact and thorough translation of this learned and elegant production into English would supply, what has long been wanted in the language, an introduction to the study of the Roman law.

349. There are two editions of the institutes, with English translations, one by Harris, published in England, and the other by Cooper, published in this country. A new edition of the latter was recently printed at Philadelphia.[2] But by far the best edition

---

[1] Two Discourses, delivered in the Middle Temple Hall, introductory to a course of lectures on general jurisprudence and the civil law, by George Long.

[2] While this work is passing through the press, a new translation of the institutes is announced as published in England, under the follow-

of the institutes, in the knowledge of the writer, is that by Blondeau, with a French translation, published at Paris, in 1839, in two volumes, with a third, containing a *chrestomathia*, or selection of texts of the Roman law." This edition contains the text as amended by the aid of modern discoveries, a number of documents illustrative of the history of the Roman law anterior to the time of Justinian, and a historical sketch of the decline of the Roman law and of its fate, both in the east and in the west.

350. The student will find the articles on the Roman law in Smith's Greek and Roman Antiquities invaluable, as an aid, throughout his whole course. These articles are, it is believed, the only writings on the Roman law in English, except the discourses of the same author,[1] in which the writer has availed himself of the critical labors of the modern German jurists.[2]

351. The utility of a study of the Roman law, and of some knowledge of its principles, may be summed up on the following grounds: —

---

ing title: — "The Institutes of Justinian. A new edition, with English Introduction, Translation, and Notes. By Thomas C. Sandars, M. A., late Fellow of Oriel College, Oxford. London: J. W. Parker & Son." In the preparation of this work, the translator has made use of Schrader's edition of the text, and has also availed himself of the new light thrown upon the subject by the recently discovered commentaries of Gaius. The work is said to be designed for general use as well as professional readers. See Westminster Review, No. 9, N. S. p. 251.

[1] See *ante*, 47, note. [2] See *ante*, 47, note, 77, note, and 139.

352. *First.* It deserves our most profound attention, as a branch of general jurisprudence. The method, in which the Roman jurists investigate a subject, some instances of which have already been given, in the examples quoted above of the controversies of the different sects or schools,[1] is admirable. Their reasons are concisely stated and exactly to the point. An advantage, which will always remain to them, is, that they had to do with the fundamentals of jurisprudence. Admirable, however, as is the method of the great jurists of Rome, their writings are not to be placed above the legal arguments of the great lawyers of more modern times. The eminent judges of England and America, in this respect, have at least shown themselves to be the equals of their Roman predecessors; while, in the amount and variety of their labors, and in the importance of the questions submitted to them, the moderns throw the ancients entirely into the shade.

353. *Second.* Many of the legal institutions of England, and of this country, have their original in the Roman law; as, for example, among others, wills, administrations, trusts, successions, special pleading. If the last-named system did not derive its origin from the Roman law, then it would seem, that the same system, in substance, must have been the growth of different ages, and of different codes of laws.

---

[1] See *ante*, 198 – 206.

354. *Third.* The principles of general jurisprudence, contained in the Roman law, and which are supposed to be the same in all civilized countries, have, in a great degree, as we have already seen, been incorporated into the common law, or rather constitute one of its original elements.

355. *Fourth.* The foundations of the legal institutions of several of the United States, as Louisiana, Florida, Texas, California, are laid directly in the Roman law. Throughout the vast regions of country embraced within the limits of these states, and which will, ere long, be covered with an enterprising and industrious population, the Roman law prevails in the same manner and to the same extent that the common law does in the other states. In Lower Canada, where the French law was established in 1663, as then administered in the tribunals of Paris, according to the custom of Paris, that code, founded in part in the Roman law, became the common law, and still continues to be so, although since abrogated in France by the new codes. In Louisiana, the laws of France and Spain, both of which are founded in the Roman law, appear to have been successively introduced, before its cession to the United States.

356. *Fifth.* The Roman law is the basis of the legal systems, and, as it were, the common law, of most of the civilized countries of Europe and America, with whom we have commercial and other

friendly intercourse, and with whom we maintain diplomatic relations. As a system of jurisprudence common to all, it is, consequently, the foundation of the international law, both public[1] and private,[2] of modern times.

---

[1] See *ante*, 342.

[2] See *ante*, 247.

CHAPTER X.

REMARKS ON THE SO-CALLED LAW OF BAILMENT.

357. THE history of what is known to English and American lawyers under the name of the law of bailment, as it touches upon and exemplifies more of the points alluded to in the foregoing pages than any other head of the common law, will be an appropriate conclusion to this brief introduction to the study of the Roman law.

358. The origin of the term *bailment*, which, like the word *bail*, is derived from the French word *bailler*, to deliver, refers back to the early part of that long period in the legal history of England, when all the proceedings in the courts of justice were in the language of the Norman conquerors. In the phraseology of the courts, the word *bailment* was used to signify a *delivery;* from this use of the term at the bar, with the general meaning which we now give to the word *delivery*, as applied to the possession of chattels, it appears gradually to have attained a more specific meaning; until at length it seems to have taken its place as an accredited branch or head of the law, to denote the

delivery of goods, by the owner of them to another person, for a particular purpose, to be restored to the owner when that purpose should have been accomplished.

359. When a delivery of this kind takes place, the receiver of the thing, called the *bailee*, becomes thereby obliged to the owner, denominated the *bailor*, for the custody of the thing, until the purpose for which it is delivered is accomplished, and also for the exercise of the proper degree of diligence and skill to accomplish that purpose. This obligation constitutes what is called the *law of bailment*. The rules relating to this subject, though mostly derived from the Roman law, probably through Bracton's treatise, have been developed in, or on the occasion of, the cases that have from time to time occurred and been adjudged; the most important and instructive of which, as well as one of the earliest, is the celebrated case of *Coggs* v. *Bernard*,[1] decided in the queen's bench in 1703.

360. In that case, it appeared, that the defendant, not being a common porter, and without any reward, undertook to remove safely several hogsheads of brandy, belonging to the plaintiff, from one cellar to another, and that in effecting the removal, he conducted the business so very negligently, that one of the casks was staved and the contents spilled. The plaintiff brought his action on the case for the

[1] 2 Ld. Raym. 909.

damage caused by the defendant's negligence, and upon the plea of not guilty, recovered a verdict. The defendant thereupon moved in arrest of judgment, on the ground, that it was not alleged in the declaration, that the defendant was a common porter, or that he was to have any reward for his pains. The case was thought to be one of great importance, and was argued before the whole court of queen's bench, consisting of Sir John Holt, chief justice, and Gould, Powys, and Powell, justices. The judges gave their opinions *seriatim* in favor of the plaintiff.

361. Gould and Powell, justices, argued the precise case before the court, upon the authority of the decided cases and the forms in the register of writs. The chief justice, however, taking a broader view, pronounced a most elaborate argument in which he went over the whole law of bailment. "I mention these things," said he, "not so much that they are all of them so necessary, in order to maintain the proposition which is to be proved, as to clear the reason of the obligation, which is upon persons in cases of trust."[1]

362. In this learned opinion, Sir John Holt, after stating the different kinds of bailments, comments upon and lays down the principles of law applicable to each class, deriving them partly from common-law sources, like his brethren, but chiefly from the

---

[1] Jones on Bailments, App. VIII.

Roman law, and referring for the latter either to Justinian's institutes, or to Bracton; who, in his treatise on the laws and customs of England, had, as we have seen, embodied and introduced, as a part of the same, all the principles of the Roman law, which he deemed applicable and pertinent.

363. From Bracton, the chief justice quotes most frequently and freely, usually with some apologetic remark. Thus, after quoting a passage, of some length, he adds:—"This Bracton, I have cited is, I confess, an old author, but in this, his doctrine is agreeable to reason, and to what the law is in other countries." Again:—"I cite this author, though I confess he is an old one, because his opinion is reasonable, and very much to my present purpose, and there is no authority in the law to the contrary." He introduces a third quotation by the remark:—"And here again I must recur to my old author." Again, after quoting from Bracton, he says:—"I do n't find this word in any other author of our law besides in this place in Bracton, which is a full authority, if it be not thought too old. But it is supported by good reason and authority." It is worthy of remark, that Sir John Holt does not suggest any doubt, as to whether the doctrines of Bracton were those of the common law of England, or that he had borrowed them from a foreign source; and that the only ground, upon which he seemed to think the authority of Bracton might be questioned, was his antiquity.

364. This judgment may be said to have established the law of bailment, substantially as it has ever since existed, in the common law of England; that is to say, regulated and governed, for the most part, by principles drawn from the Roman law.

365. It will be apparent, from the foregoing sketch, that in the English law, the subject of the care and diligence, which are required of the possessor of the goods of another, is only treated of under the head of bailment, in reference to cases where there has been a *delivery* of the goods. Thus, Blackstone defines a bailment to be "A delivery of goods in trust, upon a contract express or implied, that the trust shall be faithfully executed on the part of the bailee."[1] So Sir William Jones defines a bailment to be, "A delivery of goods on a condition expressed or implied, that they shall be restored by the bailee to the bailor, or according to his directions, as soon as the purposes for which they were bailed should be answered."[2] The same definition, in substance, making a delivery an essential part of the contract, has been repeated by all the text writers on the common law to the present time.

366. But it is manifest, at once, that cases, in which there has been a delivery of goods by the owner, are not the only ones in which the obligation of custody or diligence arises. As Sir William

---

[1] 2 Comm. 431.

[2] Jones on Bailments, 1.

Jones himself remarks, "he might easily have taken a wider field, and have extended his inquiry "to every possible case in which one man possesses for a time the goods of another;" and "that the rules are in general the same, by whatever means the goods are legally in the hands of the possessor, whether by delivery from the owner, which is a proper bailment, or from any other person, by finding, or in consequence of some distinct contract."[1] To these cases, of the obligation of custody without delivery, may be added those of the seller of goods, which are not yet delivered, and of the possession of goods by a partner or other joint proprietor.

367. The compilers of the Roman law, as contained in the collections of Justinian, had pursued a somewhat different course. Regarding the rules of law, relating to the obligation of custody and diligence, as not limited to cases, in which there had been a delivery of some physical thing, or even possession of it, but as applicable to all contracts generally, they treated of this obligation only in reference to each particular contract, in which it occurred, and inserted but two passages in the digest expressly relating to the general subject of *culpa* and *diligentia*.

368. These were both extracts from the writings of Ulpian, one of the writers most frequently resorted to, and copiously drawn upon, by the compilers of the digest. The first is a part of a much longer ex-

---

[1] Jones on Bailments, 34.

tract from the twenty-eighth book of Ulpian's work on the edict, inserted in the sixth title, *commodati vel contra*, of the thirteenth book of the digest. The fragment alluded to is the second paragraph of the fifth law of that title, known from its initial words, as the law *Si ut certo.* The second passage above referred to, known as the law *Contractus*, is taken from the twenty-ninth book of Ulpian's commentary on Sabinus, and makes the entire extract, inserted as the twenty-third law of the seventeenth title, *de diversis regulis juris antiqui*, of the fiftieth book of the digest.[1]

369. There is no branch of the Roman law, which, since the study of it in modern times, has given rise to so much controversy as the doctrine of responsibility for neglect; "a matter," to use the language of a French writer on the subject,[2] "concerning which the interpreters have lavished so many subtilties, and taught so many errors." But at the time when Heineccius and Pothier wrote their learned treatises on various topics of the Roman law, and for a long time previous, the commonly received opinion, on the continent of Europe, and especially in France, among the writers on the subject, had reduced the whole doctrine of responsibility for neglect to a system, of which the following[3] are

---

[1] Both these passages are quoted and translated by Sir William Jones in his Essay on Bailments, 15, 16.

[2] Le Brun, Essai sur la Prestation des Fautes, Preface, 1.

[3] Heineccius, Elementa Juris Civilis, sec. ord. Inst. § 784; Pothier,

the essential principles, as stated by the authors above named.

370. "When one person is in possession of things which belong or are due to another, or where one conducts affairs which are not exclusively his own, the question arises, what degree of care such person is bound to exert? In order to give an answer to this question, in the different cases that may arise, it is necessary to distinguish three sorts of diligence, and consequently three degrees or sorts of faults."

371. "The first kind of diligence is that which the most attentive persons bring to the management of their affairs; *diligentia diligentissimi patrisfamilias, exactissima diligentia.* The absence of this diligence constitutes very slight fault, *levissima culpa.*"

372. "The second kind of diligence is that which belongs to the generality of men, *diligentia mediocris seu diligentia diligenti patrisfamilias.* The absence of this diligence constitutes slight fault, *culpa levis.*"

373. "The third kind of diligence is that which the least attentive persons exhibit; the absence of which constitutes gross fault, *culpa lata.* This kind of fault consists in not bringing to the affairs of another that degree of care, which the least careful persons do not fail to exhibit in the conduct of their own affairs. This fault is assimilated to fraud, *dolus;*

Observation Generale, Œuvres (Dupin's Ed.) Tom. I. p. 553; Themis, ou Bibliotheque de Jurisconsulte, II. 349.

the commission of it is not supposed to be possible, without a breach of good faith."

374. "In order to determine for what kind of fault one is liable, or, in other words, to what kind of diligence a party is subjected, in the different contracts and quasi-contracts, three principles are applicable."

375. "The first is, that in contracts which are made for the sole interest of the creditor, the debtor is only required to observe good faith, that is to say, he is only responsible for gross neglect. To this principle, however, there are several exceptions; first, the contract of mandate; second, the quasi-contract, *negotiorum gestorum*, and third, the relation of guardianship."

376. "The second principle is, that in contracts and quasi-contracts, which are made for the reciprocal interest of the parties, such as the contracts of sale, letting to hire, pledge, partnership, and the quasi-contract of community, the debtor is liable for slight fault."

377. "The third principle is, that in contracts which are made for the sole interest of the party, who receives and is bound to restore the thing, which forms the subject of the contract, such as the contract of loan for use (*commodatum*), the debtor is responsible for the slightest fault."

378. Such was considered to be the doctrine of

the Roman law, as expounded by most of the continental jurists, at the time when Sir William Jones published his learned and elegant essay on the law of bailments; the most important effect of which was the formal introduction, into the common law, of the system just stated, namely, the three degrees of fault and of the corresponding diligence, accompanied by the three principles laid down for determining, in any given case, the degree of fault for which a party would be liable. This had not previously been done, either by any text-writer, or by Sir John Holt in his judgment in *Coggs* v. *Bernard*, or by the judges in any other decided case. Since the publication of the essay, the system of the three degrees has been the received doctrine of the common law of England and of this country; has been recognized and repeated by all the text-writers; and has been expounded and applied by courts of justice.

379. Sir William Jones thus explains the method upon which he proposed to investigate the subject:— "I propose to begin with treating the subject *analytically*, and, having traced every part of it up to the first principles of natural reason, shall proceed *historically*, to show with what perfect harmony those principles are recognized and established by other nations, especially the Romans, as well as by our English courts, when their decisions are properly understood and clearly distinguished; after which I shall resume, *synthetically*, the whole learning of *bail-*

ments, and expound such rules as, in my humble apprehension, will prevent any further perplexity on this interesting title, except in cases very peculiarly circumstanced."[1]

380. The result of this analysis, among other things, was the establishment of three degrees of neglect, and of three rules for determining which degree is applicable in any given case.

381. These principles are thus stated by the author. The degrees of neglect are as follows: —

"Ordinary neglect is the omission of that care, which every man of common prudence, and capable of governing a family, takes of his own concerns."

"Gross neglect is the want of that care, which every man of common sense, how inattentive soever, takes of his own property."

"Slight neglect is the omission of that diligence, which very circumspect and thoughtful persons use in securing their own goods and chattels."[2]

382. The rules for the application of these principles, "which," the author remarks, "may be considered as axioms flowing from natural reason, good morals, and sound policy," are laid down as follows: —

"A bailee, who derives no benefit from his undertaking, is responsible only for gross neglect."

---

[1] Jones on Bailments, 4.

[2] Id. 118.

"A bailee, who alone receives benefit from the bailment, is responsible for slight neglect."

"When the bailment is beneficial to both parties, the bailee must answer for ordinary neglect."[1]

383. It will be manifest, from a comparison of the principles above stated, as the result of the analysis, with the system of the writers on the Roman law, that the two, with some difference of phraseology, are the same in substance. It is impossible, therefore, to resist the conclusion, that the latter, as it was well known to the author of the essay, was the origin rather than the result of the analysis, and that he was in fact indebted for his system to the continental writers on the Roman law.

384. It will be recollected, that this whole system, though supposed to be drawn from the texts of the Roman law, was not in fact taught there directly in terms, and in its axiomatic form, but was the inference only, not without some dissenting voices, of the commentators and other writers on that law. Several jurisconsults had, at different periods, attempted to establish a doctrine more or less varying from it.

385. Donellus, a French writer, who was a professor of law at Heidelberg and at Leyden, in the seventeenth century, had already made the remark, that the reconciliation of the texts of the Roman law, concerning this matter, was attended with inex-

[1] Jones on Bailments, 119.

tricable difficulties; and he undertook to prove that we ought to distinguish only two degrees of fault. The same doctrine, of two degrees only, had also been maintained, at the same epoch, by Raevardus, a German author.

386. Thomasius, a professor of law in Halle, at the commencement of the last century, in a dissertation entitled, *De uso practico doctrinæ de culparum præstatione in contractibus,* maintained that the division of faults into three degrees was wholly wanting in exactness; that between what was called *slight fault* (ordinary neglect) and *very slight fault* (slight neglect), the differences were not so strongly marked or characteristic as to be justly distinguishable; that *gross fault* (neglect) was easily confounded with *fraud*, and *very slight fault* with *accident;* that the rules established by the interpreters, in consequence of this division, were subject to so many exceptions, that the latter had at length become more numerous than the rules themselves; and that the Roman jurisconsults did not agree with one another, in regard to the doctrine in question.

387. Jaques Godefroi, a lawyer of Geneva, about the middle of the seventeenth century, in his commentary on the title, *De Regulis Juris*, while he admitted three sorts of faults, distinguished them differently from other jurisconsults. But the latest adversary of the common doctrine, until the present century, was Le Brun, a French advocate, who pub-

lished his essay on responsibility for neglect,[1] about the middle of the last century.

388. In this work, the author attacks and rejects the doctrine of the three degrees; and contends that by the Roman law, there were in fact only two degrees of diligence; the one that of a provident and attentive father of a family; and the other that which the party himself is accustomed to take of his own affairs.[2] This tract, which the author sent to Pothier, was honored by the latter, says Sir William Jones,[3] with a short but complete answer, in the form of a general observation on his treatises, published at the end of his treatise on the marriage contract.[4]

389. The ideas of Thomasius, set forth in his dissertation above mentioned, it appears, exerted such an influence upon the minds of the most profound jurisconsults in Germany, that, at the present day, the system of the three degrees of fault, or three sorts of diligence, has generally given place to another system of doctrine, which seems to be not very unlike that advanced by Le Brun, and which is set

---

[1] Essai sur la Prestation des Fautes, à Paris, 1764; reprinted in 1813. In this last edition, the general observation of Pothier, in answer to the essay, is inserted; but the preface is omitted. The latter is reprinted in the Themis, VIII. 124.

[2] Jones on Bailments, 27, 28.

[3] Id. 30.

[4] Reprinted in Dupin's edition of Pothier's works, at the end of the treatise on obligations.

forth with all the desirable details in a treatise on the doctrine of *Culpa*, according to the Roman law, by J. C. Hasse, which is considered as a classic in the German universities.[1]

390. In France, the doctrine of the three degrees prevailed generally, at least in the schools of law, at the time of the promulgation of the civil code. But by the code,[2] it is provided as follows:—"The obligation to keep the thing, whether the agreement has for its object only the benefit of one of the parties, or their common benefit, renders him who is charged with it responsible for all the care of a good father of a family. This obligation is of greater or less extent, relating to certain contracts, whose effects, in this respect, are explained under the titles which concern them." In his exposition of reasons, the principal compiler of this title says, of the old system:[3]—"This division of faults is more ingenious than useful in practice. The theory, by which we divide faults into several classes, without being able to distinguish between them, cannot but diffuse a false light, and give rise to more numerous contestations." The better opinion seems to be, that the

---

[1] Die Culpa des Rœmischen Rechts, by John Christian Hasse, professor of law at Kœnigsberg. Kiel, 1815, 8vo. pp. 669. A second edition of this work has been published.

[2] Article 1137, book iii. title iii. *Of contracts and conventional obligations in general.*

[3] Bigot-Préameneu, Exposé des motifs, v. 17.

terms of the article are too express, and the ideas of the compilers too clearly explained, on this point, to leave any doubt of their intention to abrogate the ancient jurisprudence.[1]

391. From the foregoing sketch of the history of the English law of bailment, and of the Roman law on the same subject, we gather the following interesting and somewhat curious facts: —

392. (1). The common law, under the name of bailment, treats of responsibility for neglect; but only in reference to cases in which there is a delivery of goods by the owner to another person; whereas, in fact, it is entirely immaterial whether such delivery takes place or not.

393. (2). The doctrine of responsibility for neglect is applicable not only to cases in which there is a delivery or possession of some personal chattel, but also to all contracts, express or implied, for the doing of any thing for another.

394. (3). The principles of the Roman law, in reference to responsibility for neglect, have been incorporated into the common law by the authority of text-writers, and by judicial sanction, as the only

---

[1] For this statement of the system of the three degrees of fault, and the received doctrine on the subject at the present day, in Germany and France, I am indebted, in part, to an article by M. Blondeau, reviewing La Brun's essay above-mentioned, (*ante*, 387), in the Themis, II. 349. The work of Le Brun is also reviewed by Hasse, in the Zeitschrift fur Geschichtlihe Rechtswissenchaft, Band IV. 189.

existing principles of law relating and applicable to the subject.

395. (4.) The system of the three degrees of neglect or fault, which was in vogue on the continent of Europe, at the middle of the last century, and at that time taught by the commentators on the Roman law, as the fair result of its doctrines, was introduced into the common law of England and of this country, in which it still prevails, by the sole authority of Sir William Jones, by the publication of his essay on the law of bailments.

396. (5). This system, it appears, has been since abrogated in France by the new civil code, and is now generally abandoned in Germany, as the result of a more careful study, and a sounder criticism, of the sources of the Roman law.

397. (6). The establishment of this system in the common law, as the doctrine and on the authority of the Roman law, when it was in fact not taught there, but was the mistaken inference therefrom of the writers on the subject, furnishes an apt example of one of the principal objections, — the then imperfect state of legal science, — of the German historical school, to the plan of codification proposed by Thibaut.[1]

398. (7). The doctrine of the three degrees, according to Sir William Jones's analysis,[2] when "traced up to the first principles of natural reason,"

---

[1] See *ante*, 271, 272.

[2] Jones on Bailments, 4, 11.

consisting of the "plain elements" of natural law, it will not be without interest to contrast with this statement the opinion of a German jurist,[1] quoted by Hasse, in the preface to his work on the *Culpa* of the Roman law, as to his experience of the practical value and importance of the doctrine: — "This matter (the doctrine of the degrees of *culpa*), is of more account in the schools than in the forum; since in civil life, the inquiry most frequently arises, not as to the degree of *culpa*, but as to its existence, or whether, on the whole, any *culpa* has been committed. In my whole six-and-thirty years' practice, I do not remember a single case, in which the parties had any controversy concerning the degree of *culpa*."

---

[1] Titius ad Lauterbach. obs. 102.

APPENDIX.

TABLE

OF THE RUBRICS OF THE SEVERAL TITLES OF THE INSTITUTES, DIGEST, AND CODE, ARRANGED IN ALPHABETICAL ORDER.

A.

Ad legem Corneliam de sicariis. D. 48, 8. C. 9, 16.
Ad legem Fabiam de plagiariis. C. 9, 20. D. 48, 15.
Ad legem Falcidiam. D. 35, 2. C. 6, 50. I. 2, 22.
Ad legem Juliam de adulteriis. D. 48, 5. C. 9, 9.
Ad legem Juliam de ambitu. C. 9, 26. D. 48, 14.
Ad legem Juliam majestatis. D. 48, 4. C. 9, 8.
Ad legem Juliam peculatus, etc. D. 48, 13. C. 9, 28.
Ad legem Juliam repetundarum. C. 9, 27. D. 48, 11.
Ad legem Juliam de vi publica. D. 48, 6. C. 9, 12.
Ad legem Juliam de vi privata. D. 48, 7. C. 9, 12.
Ad legem Viselliam. C. 9. 21.
de Administratione et periculo tutorum et curatorum, etc. D. 26, 7.
de Administratione rerum ad civitates pertinentium. D. 50, 8.
de Administratione rerum publicarum. C. 11, 30.
de Administratione tutorum vel curatorum, etc. C. 5, 37.
Ad municipalem et de incolis. D. 50, 1.
de Adoptionibus. I. 1, 11. C. 8, 48.
de Adoptionibus et emancipationibus, etc. D. 1, 7.
Ad SC. Macedonianum. C. 4, 28. D. 14, 6.
Ad SC. Orphitianum. I. 3, 4. C. 6, 57. D. 38, 17.
Ad SC. Tertullianum. I. 3, 3. C. 6, 56. D. 38, 17.
Ad SC. Trebellianum. D. 36, 1. C. 6, 49.
Ad SC. Turpillianum, etc. D. 48, 16. C. 9, 42, 45.
Ad SC. Velleianum. D. 16, 1. C. 4, 29.
de Advocatis diversorum judiciorum. C. 2, 7.
de Advocatis diversorum judicum. C. 2, 8.
de Advocatis fisci. C. 2, 9.
de Ædificiis privatis. C, 8, 10.
de Ædilitiis actionibus. C. 4, 58.
de Ædilitio edicto, etc. D. 21, 1.
de Æstimatoria actione. D. 19, 3.
de Agentibus in rebus. C. 12, 20.
de Agnoscendis et alendis liberis, etc. D. 25, 3. C. 5, 25.
de Agricolis, et censitis, et colonis. C. 11, 47.
de Agricolis et mancipiis dominicis, etc. C. 11, 67.
de Albo scribendo. D. 50, 3.
de Aleatoribus. D. 11, 5. C. 3, 43.
de Alendis liberis ac parentibus. C. 5, 25. D. 25, 3.
de Alexandriæ primatibus. C. 11, 28.

18

B.

C.

D.

F.

G.

H.

I.

J.

L.

M.

N.

O.

P.

R.

S.

Sine censu vel reliquis fundum comparari non posse. C. 4, 47.
de Singulis rebus per fideicommissum relictis. I. 2, 24.
Si nuptiæ ex rescripto petantur. C. 5, 8.
Si omissa sit causa testamenti. C. 6, 39.
Si pars hereditatis petatur. D. 5, 4.
Si pendente appellatione mors intervenerit. D. 49, 13. C. 7, 66.
Si per vim vel alio modo absentis turbata sit possessio. C. 8, 5.
Si pignoris conventionem numeratio pecuniæ secuta non sit. C. 8, 33.
Si pignus pignori datum sit. C. 8, 24.
Si plures una sententia condemnati sunt. C. 7, 55.
Si post creationem quis decesserit. C. 10, 68.
Si propter inimicitias creatio facta sit. C. 10, 66.
Si propter publicas pensitationes venditio fuerit celebrata. C. 4, 46.
Si quacunque præditus potestate, etc., ad suppositarum jurisdictioni suæ adspirare tentaverint nuptias. C. 5, 7.
Si quadrupes pauperiem fecisse dicatur. I. 4, 9. D. 9, 1.
Si quid in fraudem patroni factum sit. D. 38, 5. C. 6, 5.
Si quis aliquem testari prohibuerit vel coegerit. D. 29, 6. C. 6, 34.
Si quis alteri, vel sibi sub alterius nomine, vel aliena pecunia emerit. C. 4, 50.
Si quis cautionibus in judicio sistendi causa factis non obtemperaverit. D. 2, 11.
Si quis eam, cujus tutor fuerit, corruperit. C. 9, 10.
Si quis ignorans rem minoris esse sine decreto comparaverit. C. 5, 73.
Si quis Imperatori maledixerit. C. 9, 7.
Si quis in jus vocatus non ierit, etc. D. 2, 5.
Si quis jus dicenti non obtemperaverit. D. 2, 3.
Si quis omissa causa testamenti ab intestato, etc., possidet hereditatem. D. 29, 4.
Si rector provinciæ, vel ad eum, pertinentes, sponsalitia dederint. C. 5, 2.
Si reus vel accusator mortuus fuerit. C. 9, 6.
Si sæpius in integrum restitutio postuletur. C. 2, 44.
Si secundo nupserit mulier, cui maritus usumfructum reliquit. C. 5, 10.
Si servitus vindicetur, vel ad alium pertinere negetur. D. 8, 5.

U.

V.

INDEX.

The numbers refer to the paragraphs.

ERRATA.

Page 126, last line, the reference should be to paragraph 296.
" 128, last line, before *International* insert *Private*.